HEADSTART HISTORY PAPERS

John Dudley, Duke of Northumberland:
Lord President of the Council

By

David Loades

HEADSTART HISTORY

Copyright   David Loades 1996

All rights reserved. No production, copy or transmission of this publication may be made without written permission. No paragraph may be reproduced copied or transmitted without such permission or in accordance with the provisions of the Copyright Act 1956 as amended. Any person who does any unauthorised act in relation to this publication is liable to criminal prosecution and civil claim for damages.

Published by Headstart History
108 St Aldates Oxford OX1 1BU

Printed by   JUMA, Sheffield

ISBN 1 873041 80 2

Sales: Four Seasons House
102B Woodstock Road, Witney
Oxfordshire OX8 6DY GB.

Illustration: Warwick Castle

CONTENTS

Introduction

1	Prologue	1
II	Emergence	3
III	The making of a courtier	8
IV	Viscount Lisle 1540-1543	13
V	The Lord High Admiral 1543-1547	18
VI	The Earl of Warwick 1547-1549	24
VII	The reins of power 1549-1550	36
VIII	Lord President of the Council	47
IX	The fall of the Duke of Northumberland 1552-1553	67
	Notes and References	83
	Further reading: books	85
	articles	86

Introduction

The **Headstart History Papers** aim to identify themes and topics the significance of which extends beyond the studies of professional historians. The Papers are distillations of the research of distinguished scholars in a form appropriate to students and the general reader.

John Dudley has not had a good press. Within a few weeks of his fall Robert Wingfield described him as '...an amibitious man descended of an ambitious father'. Wingfield was not writing history, but propaganda on behalf of Mary. However, his verdict stood, and half a century later John Hayward, who had no reason to defend the queen, nevertheless wrote of Dudley 'He was of great spirit and highly aspiring, not forbearing to make any mischief the meanes of attaining his ambitious endes...' This character, of a good soldier marred by greed and unscrupulous ambition, was transmitted by the seventeenth century historians, Fuller, Strype, and Burnet, to Froude and Pollard who brought it into the twentieth century. There were two main reasons for this. In the first place Dudley was, understandably, given the whole blame for the unsuccessful bid to alter the succession in 1553; a bid which, if it had succeeded, would seriously have undermined the newly established ascendancy of statute, by which later generations were to set such store. Secondly, by renouncing the protestant faith of which he had appeared to be such an energetic protagonist, he foreited the rehabilitation which Elizabeth and her successors accorded to most of Mary's victims. In other words he ended up with the worst of both worlds.

This situation was aggravated by the mythology which grew up around the Duke of Somerset. Because of his supposed sympathy with the exploited commons, Somerset became 'the good duke' both in his own lifetime and to subsequent generations. The 'bad duke' antithesis for Northumberland became irresistable, and was reinforced in the present century by the socialist convictions of such distinguished economic historians as R.H.Tawney. Even W.K.Jordan, writing in the 1960s who was well aware of Somerset's limitations, subscribed to this mythical contrast. His otherwise admirable books on the reign of Edward VI are laced with pejorative comments on the competence and integrity of the Duke of Northumberland which are frequently at odds with the evidence which he is presenting.

Only within the last twenty five years had a serious reappraisal of Dudley's career and reputation been attempted. In 1973 Barrett Beer argued that he was less a villain than a pragmatist who was forced eventually into a political gamble which failed. Since then Dale Hoak has contrasted his style of government favourably with that of the Protector, a verdict also endorsed by Michael Bush. Glyn Parry has specifically demythologised the 'good duke'. Most recently David Loades has explored the whole career of the Duke of Northumberland in a new book published by the OUP. This Paper is a summary of the main conclusions in that book in which you will find a guide to the motives and achievement of this fascinating political figure.

Judith Loades
Oxford, St Giles Day, 1996

John Dudley; Earl of Warwick and Duke of Northumberland

1 Prologue

By the early fifteenth century it had been fully established that only the king could create or promote a peer; and although a peerage could be resigned on grounds such as poverty, it could only be removed by attainder. Attainder was a formal process of law, but it was also a judicial weapon in the hands of the king. When Edward IV personally accused his brother the Duke of Clarence of High Treason, his attainder was a foregone conclusion. A peer was therefore uniquely accessible to the royal pleasure or displeasure, and this vulnerability was emphasised by the discontinuities which afflicted the great majority of established peerage families during the late fifteenth century. The FitzAlan Earls of Arundel, the Talbot Earls of Shrewsbury and the Nevill Earls of Westmorland were the only major peers whose titles ran without a break from before 1450 to the death of Henry VIII. Before 1520 this was more the result of accident than of deliberate policy. Edward IV restored the Percy Earls of Northumberland in 1470; Henry VII restored the Stafford Dukes of Buckingham and the de Vere Earls of Oxford in 1485; and Henry VIII restored the Courtenay Earls of Devon and the Plantagenet Earls of Salisbury in 1511 and 1513. Other examples could be cited. But after 1520 the king's attitude began to change. Buckingham, Exeter and Salisbury were all destroyed by attainder on flimsy grounds, and Northumberland was persuaded into a voluntary surrender.

Under the pressure of an uncertain succession and self-induced political crisis, Henry ceased to be impressed by ancient blood, and came to see his peers chiefly as his own servants and agents. Early in his reign he had elevated personal favourites such as Sir Charles Brandon for no discernable strategic reason, but from about 1525 onward all his creations either had a political purpose, or were rewards for political and administrative services. In the last twenty years of the reign there were a number of peers who were soldiers, but no more warriors became peers.

Although the character of such an established institution could not be changed within one generation, the shift of emphasis was significant. The Boleyn, Manners, Radcliffe and Hastings creations between 1525 and 1533 were all rewards for support in an increasingly difficult situation. Seymour, Parr, Cromwell, Russell and Dudley were similarly elevated partly for their loyalty to Henry personally, and partly for their value as agents of government. By 1547 the service nobility was dominant, and even the Duke of Norfolk, in the last year or two before his fall, did not presume to display a power base outside the court. Those peers who still retained great 'manred' in their countries, such as the Earls of Shrewsbury and Derby, kept quiet about it and were as assiduous as their more parvenue colleagues in demonstrating their devotion to the Tudors. Consequently the men who ran England during Edward VI's minority were the service peers whom his father had created. As the Princess Mary correctly observed in 1551 '..my father made the more part of you almost from nothing'.[1] They promoted themselves, and co-opted other men of the same type to join them. They exercised great power, and were free for the most part from personal vulnerability to a wayward king. But they knew (or thought they knew) that Edward's majority was only a matter of time, and manoeuvred assiduously to control the court and council when that moment should come. In this John Dudley was conspicuously successful, but he was a creature of his generation and circumstances. When he failed to control the Crown, through circumstances over which he had no control, he had no position to fall back on. Neither his great wealth nor his ostensible power could protect him, because both were political artefacts of recent development, rooted only in the institutions at Westminster. Dudley was not an over mighty subject. He was a politician whose whole position ultimately rested upon his ability to retain the confidence of the monarch. In that he looked back to Thomas Wolsey and Thomas Cromwell rather than to the magnates of earlier generations; and his spiritual heir was Robert Devereux, Earl of Essex.

II Emergence

John Dudley was born in 1504, the eldest son of Edmund Dudley and his second wife, Elizabeth, the sister and co-heir of John, Lord Lisle. Edmund's father was John Dudley of Atherington, Sussex, the second son of John Sutton, Lord Dudley. Young John was thus on the fringes of the peerage through both his parents, but the most important thing about his father was not his proximity to a barony but the fact that he was, by the time that his first son was born, a highly trusted servant of king Henry VII. Edmund and Sir Richard Empson were the two 'judices fiscales', trained lawyers whose job it was to locate and exploit situations in which the king could increase his occasional revenue. In other words to manipulate the fiscal prerogative.[2] There is no doubt that the king drove this policy, but it was so widely and deeply unpopular that his subjects were unwilling to place the responsibility where it belonged. Consequently by the time that Henry died in April 1509 it was conveniently believed that Empson and Dudley were his evil geniuses. Within a few days both had been arrested, and since it would have been impossible in law to charge them with any offence for actions which they had carried out on the king's explicit instructions, an elaborate fiction was constructed. Edmund was accused of assembling men and gathering arms at his house in Candlewick Street, London, for the purpose of kidnapping the young king and seizing control of the government. It would be hard to imagine a more far-fetched ambition, but the plausibility of the intention was irrelevant. Edmund probably did assemble a small band of armed men, fearing that the king's death would provide a signal for some of his numerous enemies to take the law into their own hands. Since Henry VIII had actually retained the majority of his father's councillors and servants in post, he needed an eye catching gesture to make it appear that he was making a fresh start. Consequently Edmund Dudley was tried and convicted of High Treason on the 18th July 1509, and Sir Richard Empson on the 2nd October. The young king may have hoped that this would be sufficient, for the condemned men remained in prison until August of the following year, but a certain inexorable logic forced him to carry out the sentences. His father's fiscal policy had undoubtedly been oppressive, and sometimes unjust, a matter which must either remain as a burden upon his successor's conscience, or be discharged by transferring the guilt to the obvious scapegoats. Edmund protested vigorously against the injustice of the sentence which had been passed upon him, but was not unwilling to discharge his own and his master's conscience by laying down his life. He was executed on the 17th August 1510.

All his children were under six at the time of his arrest, and presumably remained with their mother, although where that may have been is not apparent. On the 12th November 1511 Elizabeth remarried, her second husband being Arthur Plantagenet, the illegitimate son of King Edward IV. Shortly after Arthur was granted such of Edmund Dudley's lands as still remained in the hands of the Crown, but there was no mention of the wardship of his heir, or indeed of any of his children. At some point, probably at the time of her remarriage, Elizabeth seems to have transferred the custody of John to Edward Guildford, a well connected Esquire of the Body. Whether this was a voluntary arrangement or imposed as the result of a dispute, we do not know. In February 1512 Guildford was formally granted his wardship, and John himself was restored in blood '...being not yet eight years old'.**3** His father's attainder was annulled by statute. It is unlikely that he grew up with more than the vaguest memory of his father, and Edmund's fate would have cast very little shadow. In later life, when he had become both important and unpopular, people remembered that his father had died a traitor; but at the time it was realized that Edmund had been a political sacrifice, and the rapid rehabilitation of his heir was a recognition of that fact. Later there were to be hints that Arthur Plantagenet felt that he should have received the wardship but at the time Guildford was a more promising guardian, and at the age of seven John would probably have left the immediate care of his mother anyway. In the short term Guildford's reward for his care was probably modest, as most of the Dudley inheritance had been alienated before the wardship was granted, but he would have received the profits of those lands which Edmund had already enfeoffed to John's use before his attainder. Edward Guildford was a close friend of Charles Brandon, served in the French campaign of 1513, and was knighted at the seige of Tournai. His principal seat was at Halden in Kent, and it was there that young John Dudley grew from childhood to adolescence. Nothing is known about that process, but some things can be deduced. There is no sign of him having attended any institution of education, neither school, university nor Inn of Court. It is therefore reasonable to suppose that he was educated by a tutor in Sir Edward's household, along with his own children, Richard and Jane. That would have been normal for the son of an important gentleman at that time. Sir Henry Wyatt had been altogether exceptional in sending his son Thomas to Cambridge. John's schooling seems to have been conventional and undistinguished. In later life he was literate in English, but professed to understand no latin, probably because he had forgotten the little which he had once learned. He had no known intellectual interests, and did not patronise conventional scholars. He was to show an interest in practical sciences such as cartography and navigation, but it is very unlikely that he acquired that interest during his childhood. He was not brought up to follow his father into the law, but to follow his guardian as a courtier and soldier. By the summer of 1514 Sir Edward had become Master of the Tower Armoury, and ex officio judge and master of ceremonies for the king's jousts, at that time a very high profile aspect of court life. At the age of thirteen John would have been old enough to have accompanied him to court, and made himself useful as a page, although there is no conclusive evidence that he did so. Richard may have been a sickly or unpromising youth. He was to predecease his father, and John seems to have been treated from the beginning as Sir Edward's own son. At what point he became betrothed to Jane Guildford is not known, nor whether such a betrothal corresponded with his own wishes, but it was probably before he attained his eighteenth birthday, and the subsequent marriage was a happy one.

In 1519 Sir Edward was appointed Knight Marshall of Calais, possibly a move by Wolsey to distance him from the court, although for what reason is not apparent. John may have accompanied him. The young man's first independent appearance came in 1521, when as a youth of seventeen he joined the Cardinal's retinue during the latter's abortive attempt to mediate between France and the Empire. This would have been a purely educational trip - he was given no sort of responsibility - but it marked his first small step in public life. In the following year, as war with France approached again, Sir Edward seems to have given his young protege a very junior command among the soldiers of the Calais garrison, and he probably gained his first military experience in the skirmishing which took place around the fringes of the Pale towards the end of that year. When the Duke of Suffolk led an English army to France in September 1523, Sir Edward Guildford was among his officers, and John Dudley accompanied him. It was not a successful campaign, but Sir Edward distinguished himself at the capture of Bohen on the 14th November, and on the 7th of the same month the Duke knighted Dudley, then aged nineteen.[4] It is possible that he may have done this as a favour to his old friend, because there is no record of any feat of gallantry which might otherwise have prompted it. Suffolk was generous with knighthoods during this campaign, but he could hardly have bestowed the honour on anyone who was obviously unworthy, and Dudley was probably showing, at the very outset of his career, that combination of courage and audacity which was to be characteristic of him in later life.

III The Making of a courtier, 1523-1540

There were to be no further opportunities for glory, as the war fizzled out, but by the end of 1524 Sir John Dudley was back at court, as a Esquire of the Body. Since the rise of the Privy Chamber this was no longer a position which implied close proximity to the king, but it was a place of honour, and during the Christmas festivities of that year Dudley appeared prominently among the jousters, which was always a sign of royal favour. In 1525 he attained his majority, but because he was not required to sue livery, there is no record of exactly what he inherited. He would also have received some lands as a jointure for his wife because he must have married Jane at about the same time. She reached the age of sixteen in 1525, and since they had produced at least two, and probably three children by 1528, they must have married as soon as he reached the age of twenty one.**5** There is no record of where they lived at this stage, but it was probably upon one of his manors in Surrey or Sussex. Sir John remained principally a courtier, and made no mark in local affairs. He did not even appear upon a commission of the peace until 1531. Apart from Guildford, Dudley had no patron, and this was to prove an advantage during the difficult years ahead. He was sufficiently favoured by Wolsey to join the massive entourage which he took to France in 1527, but he was never in the Cardinal's service, and was unaffected by his fall in 1529. Like his guardian, Dudley was the king's man, and although he was to play an active part in the politics of the court, his alignment was always to be determined principally by his reading of

Henry's mind. This was hazardous, and he sometimes made mistakes, but he never suffered from divided loyalties. To what extent this was altruistic may be doubted. Self interest dictated that a courtier should study the royal mood with extreme care, but such was also his duty, and excessive cynicism about Dudley's motives would not be justified.

At some point between 1525 and 1528 his mother, Lady Elizabeth Plantagenet, died. This should have conferred upon John the barony of Lisle, but Elizabeth's second husband, Arthur Plantagenet, had already been created Viscount Lisle in 1523, and his right was neither claimed nor recognised. Whether he inherited any property directly from his mother is not clear. Lord Lisle had a life interest in the bulk of her estate, and the real issue of the inheritance only arose after his death, but there are so few records of Dudley in the late 1520s that it is not possible to conclude that he received nothing at that time. He sold some lands in Hampshire in 1527, but whether they had been obtained in this way, or were part of his own patrimony, or had been previously purchased, is not clear. Noone commented upon Sir John's behaviour during the critical years between 1528 and 1532, when the court was becoming increasingly divided over the king's Great Matter. This may have been because he was not sufficiently important to attract attention, or he may have been keeping a deliberately low profile as he tracked Henry's uncertain and frustrated course. Whichever was the case, he had emerged by 1532, unsurprisingly, as an ally of the Boleyns and an associate of Thomas Cromwell.

In March 1532 Sir John obtained his first office, a grant of the constableship of Warwick castle, jointly in survivorship with the established favourite, Sir Francis Bryan.6 A number of other offices were granted with the constableship, giving an annual fee of about £45, and enough status in the county for him to be added to the Warwickshire commission of the Peace later in the year. Quite suddenly, and probably as a result of his relationship with Cromwell, the mists which had shrouded so much of Dudley's early life began to lift. He obtained his first wardship, that of Anthony Norton of Worcestershire, and stood surety for a substantial sum which Sir Edward Seymour had borrowed from the king. During the same year he also entered into a complex financial relationship with his kinsman, Lord Dudley. The latter was deep in debt, partly because of his father's extravagance, and partly as a result of his own incompetence. John loaned him £1400, for which he bound himself to repay £2000 over five years, on the security of a portion of his lands. Dudley was soon in difficulties over his repayments, and complaining vigorously to Cromwell. Sir John was not his only creditor, but he was the most important, because in addition to the £1400, he also seems to have given Dudley a mortgage on the remained of his estate for £6000. By 1533 the wretched peer was totally mired, and four years later had sold the entire estate, including Dudley castle, to a London syndicate 'to the use of Sir John Dudley'. Lord Dudley's misfortune made him a laughing stock, and he became known as the 'lord Quondam'. He was bitterly resentful of what he considered to be Sir John's sharp practice but it does not appear that the latter behaved fraudulently, or even particularly harshly. What he did do was take advantage of his cousin's weakness to drive a hard bargain to his own advantage. His ethics were those of business rather than of traditional kindred. The remarkable aspect of the story is not that Sir John behaved in such a fashion, but that a minor courtier, with no major office or great patrimony, should have had access to such substantial capital sums. Good connections in the City of

London, and the warm breath of political favour would seem to be the answer. By 1540 he had moved his principal seat from Sussex to Worcestershire, and was known as Sir John Dudley of Dudley; but he continued to spend most of his time in or around the court.

His father-in-law, Sir Edward Guildford, died in 1535, and Sir John was quickly at loggerheads with John Guildford, his nephew and heir. Cromwell arbitrated the quarrel, and it is not clear how much Dudley gained on his wife's behalf, but the episode reveals that he was not the man to neglect the smallest opportunity for lawful profit or advantage. He had already sold much of his reversionary interest in his mother's lands, and seems to have little sense of 'country', another characteristic which cut him off from what might be described as traditional aristocratic values. In 1534 he took Sir Edward's seat as a knight of the shire for Kent, but two years later he had sold most of his lands in the county to Cromwell, and was buying vigorously in Staffordshire and the Welsh Marches. Dudley's debt to Cromwell was both financial and political, but it did not bring him any major preferment. In 1534 he took over his father in law's former office at the Tower armoury, and in 1537 secured the honourable, if not particularly significant position of King's Chief Trencher, at £50 a year. He had been pencilled in for the Vice Chamberlainship, but either Cromwell changed his mind, or the king thought differently. His attachment to the Secretary enabled him to survive the dramatic events of the spring and summer of 1536 without difficulty. However much he may have supported the Boleyn marriage in 1533, he had distanced himself from that faction before Anne's fall. In the autumn of 1536 he served at the head of 200 Sussex men against the Pilgrimage of Grace, but saw no action. There had been peace since 1525 and the nearest thing to active service would have been garrison duty in Calais or Berwick, neither an attractive prospect for an ambitious courtier, but early in 1537 he was given a new and different opportunity. In January he was commissioned as Vice Admiral, and instructed to 'keep' the Narrow Seas with a fleet of four or five ships'.[7] This meant mainly hunting for pirates, and although his voyage of about six weeks seems to have resulted in only one capture, the king was pleased with his service, and he seems to have found it congenial. Whether he had ever been to sea before cannot be ascertained. It was normal to give soldiers command of fighting ships, but Sir John's only experience of action had been fourteen years before, and it is not known that he had ever commanded a significant force in battle. In July he was sent out again, and this time won a pitched battle against several Breton ships which he caught in Mount's Bay. Whether these were actually pirates was a moot point, but Dudley had now blooded himself as a naval commander, and made a good impression on everyone who knew the business. However, there was no war in the offing, and for the time being he had to content himself with more mundane affairs. In October he attended the christening of Henry's long awaited heir, Prince Edward, and shortly after was sent to Spain in the retinue of Sir Thomas Wyatt, ambassador to the Emperor. His role in that mission was a subordinate one, and by the end of 1538 there are some signs that he was becoming frustrated by his failure to break through into any major office or honour. He was by this time a very considerable landholder; a man of substance and a familiar figure at court, apparently in the confidence of both the king and Cromwell, and yet he seemed to be unable to turn these advantages to significant effect. The post of Master of the Horse to Henry's new queen, Anne of Cleves, in December 1539, was not the promotion he was looking for. He had begun to acquire monastic property, which was a sign of special favour at this early date, and jousted again before the king at Easter 1540, but his political career seemed to have ground to a halt.

IV Viscount Lisle, 1540-1543

Cromwell's fall in June 1540 must have felt at first like the *quietus est*, but in fact Dudley's lack of success may well have protected him. Victorious in council, the conservatives were unwilling, or unable, to root out those numerous friends and sympathisers with whom Cromwell had populated the court over the previous eight years, and Sir John's 'reforming' connections did not deprive him of the king's favour. He kept a low profile for a few months, and may have retreated to the country. He had by this time six or seven surviving children, of whom the eldest, Henry, was about fourteen, and we know remarkably little about how he was bringing them up. By the end of 1541 Sir John was back at court, where he gave close support to Archbishop Cranmer in the unravelling of Queen Catherine Howard's salacious misdemeanours. The arrest and continued imprisonment of his stepfather Lord Lisle on suspicion of papist sympathies may have been a minor embarrassment, because their relations had been quite good over the last few years, but no one was likely to suspect Dudley of sharing those sympathies, and Lisle's death in prison in March 1542 was to provide him with the break through for which he yearned. Nine days after that event, on the 12th March, he was created Viscount Lisle '...by the right of his mother, Lady Elizabeth, sister and heir to Sir John Grey, Viscount Lisle, who was late wife to Arthur Plantagenet,

Viscount Lisle, deceased.' Ironically, Dudley's elevation therefore owed nothing directly to his service or his wealth, although it is unlikely that his title would have been recognised if he had not been *persona grata*. In spite of the wording used, Sir John's title was conferred by patent, and was therefore a new creation, but at the same time he was styled Baron Malpas and Lord Basset of Tyass. Neither of these titles were granted, and it is not clear where they came from. They must have been transmitted by his mother, but Arthur Plantagenet had never used them.

No chief minister took Thomas Cromwell's place, and the king's favour no longer ran through a single principal channel. This did not make the politics of the court any less tense, but it did make them more open, and for the last five years of the reign two parties confronted each other in rough equilibrium. On the one side stood the vanquishers of Cromwell; the Howard affinity, led by the Duke of Norfolk, and the religious conservatives, headed by Stephen Gardiner, bishop of Winchester. The latter group was not coherent, and did not always see eye to eye with the former, but they were generally in alliance. On the other side stood Cromwell's friends and pupils, such as Lord Audley, Sir William Paget and Sir Anthony Denny. Overlapping with this group were the religious reformers, led by Archbishop Cranmer. It would be premature to label these men as protestants, because they operated within the limits of the king's tolerance, which did not extend to heresy; but most of them were to emerge as such after his death. Edward Seymour, Earl of Hertford, the brother of Henry's third queen, Jane, and uncle to the heir to the throne, was not a natural ally of the reformers. Jane had been, if anything, on the conservative side. But Edward was closest to the king, and probably read his mind better than most. After his sixth and final marriage in the summer of 1543 to the docile but strong minded Catherine Parr, Hertford scented a shift in the wind. The advantage continued to vacillate backwards and forwards, and as late as 1546 the conservatives could still score limited victories, but slowly the reformers gained the upper hand; and having joined them, Hertford soon emerged as a leader. Whether his religious conversion was a cause or an effect of this move is not clear, but after 1547 he was to emerge as a committed and genuine protestant.

Lord Lisle followed the same course, although he was able to keep a somewhat lower profile. His relationship with Cromwell had certainly extended to support for his religious policy, and that was no doubt the chief reason for his discreet withdrawal in the latter part of 1540. In 1553 he was to describe himself as having followed the same course for sixteen years, which would date his decision to 1537. Whether his faith was ever anything more than opportunism may be debated. His cautious but increasingly firm commitment to the reforming party in the 1540s would be consistent with either interpretation. Henry's personal regard for his last wife, and his continued confidence in Cranmer, were the strongest cards in the reformers' hands. Experience and length of service favoured the conservatives, and had the period been one of peace, that might have been decisive. However it was not a period of peace. After a brief interlude of friendship in 1538-9, which had posed a serious threat to English security, Charles V and Francis I were again squaring up to each other, and Henry saw the possibility of advantage to himself in the forthcoming conflict. By the summer of 1542 he was also looking for a way back after the personal humiliation of Catherine Howard's adolescent infidelities. A victorious campaign offered an attractive way of restoring his self confidence, and re-kindling the fires of youth. So in June he negotiated an alliance with the Emperor, and began to prepare for war.

Part of that preparation was to defuse the auld alliance. Henry may have been remembering what had happened in 1513, or he may have borne a grudge against James V for snubbing his attempts to woo the Scots into the anti-papal camp. For whatever reason, even before his alliance with the Emperor was complete, he seems to have decided upon a pre-emptive strike in the north. In April 1542 Lisle was joined in commission with Sir Robert Southwell to inspect the fortifications at Berwick, and to take order for the defence of the marches. By September Henry had assembled an army in Northumberland, and was threatening the Scots with impossible demands for compensation over border infringements which were either exaggerated or invented. Before the Scottish commissioners could even consider a response, the Duke of Norfolk led his force across the border and cut a swathe of destruction through the Scottish lowlands. In terms of English domestic politics, the first advantage of the war went to the conservatives, because although Hertford had taken part in the campaign, the commanders were the Dukes of Norfolk and Suffolk. Lisle was probably being prepared for a last minute diplomatic initiative in France, which would also suggest conservative ascendancy at court, but the king, in his unpredictable way, decided otherwise. On the 8th November, when he was probably in his 39th year, Viscount Lisle was appointed Warden General of the Scottish marches.**9** This was his first major responsibility, and it came at a time of unique opportunity. James, as Henry had no doubt calculated, could not afford to ignore the provocation offered by Norfolk's raid. Toward the end of November he launched a hastily assembled host of about 20,000 men into the debatable land north of Carlisle. It was a carefully prepared trap. Within a few days the Scots had been caught and routed at Solway Moss by a much smaller but better equipped English force, and a large number of Scottish lords and gentlemen were taken prisoner. Lord Lisle had barely taken up his post when the news of this victory reached him. He could claim no share of the credit, but was immediately confronted with the necessity to assess and exploit the resulting situation. Within a few days the Scottish defeat had been turned to disaster by the death of James V, already a sick man before the battle, and the accession to the throne of his week old daughter, Mary.

So confused was the situation that Lisle hardly knew from day to day who he was dealing with, but his reports, many of which survive, show a shrewd political mind, and considerable energy. It was Henry who decided to press for a marriage treaty, betrothing the infant queen to his own five year old son; a policy designed in the short term to break down Scotland's links with France, and in the longer term to unite the kingdoms under English rule. However it was Lisle who began to build up a pro-English party in Edinburgh to support the 'assured lords' - those Scottish prisoners who had agreed to purchase their liberty by supporting the marriage. Lisle did not bring off any notable coup during his five months or so in the borders, but he did succeed in working with the Scottish council, and in recruiting a number of lowland lairds to the English cause. The king was pleased, and in January 1543, while he was still deeply enmeshed in the affairs of the north, Viscount Lisle was appointed Lord Admiral. In less than a year he had progressed from middle ranking courtier to great officer of state, and although the context was military, he had commanded no force in the field, and had probably not heard a shot fired in anger.

V The Lord High Admiral, 1543-1547

As Lord Admiral, Lisle became an ex officio member of the Privy Council, but because he was not immediately relieved of his responsibilities in the north, he did not take his seat until April. He was sworn on the 23rd of that month, and on the same day became a knight of the Garter.10 It would probably be true to say that he had so far shown no spectacular talent, and that these rewards had been earned by assiduity and loyalty. The king trusted him. As Lord Admiral, however, he was a conspicuous success. In 1543 Henry had had a standing navy for over twenty years, and had overseen a number of important developments in ship design and gunnery. However, naval administration had evolved only patchily, and had failed to keep pace with the scale and complexity of the operation. Naval tactics had hardly evolved at all, and the fleet orders issued by Lord Audley in 1530 still envisaged a series of unco-ordinated combats between individual ships. dDuring the four years in which Lisle held the office there were significant advances on both fronts. In 1545 the four existing officers of the navy were augmented to seven, and formed into a Council for Marine causes, with a defined departmental autonomy and proper line management. Whether this reorganisation was Lisle's idea, or whether he was acting upon suggestions originating with the king, or Thomas Cromwell, we do not know, but he had the executive responsibility for carrying it out, and the result was the most effective naval administration in Europe. At the same time the fleet orders which he issued in the same year showed a revolution in thinking since 1530. Lisle envisaged a fleet divided into squadrons, co-ordinated manoeuvring and synchronised gunfire. This was not original thinking, but it did show an awareness of current Spanish and Portuguese theory which was most unusual among English seamen or commanders at that time. It seems that Lisle's previous experience of naval service in 1537 had given him an enthusiasm for the sea which not only made him a most suitable Lord Admiral but informed a number of his other actions and attitudes.

In 1543 he made a slow start. Not only was he detained on the borders, but the king also continued to be preoccupied with Scottish affairs. In July he signed the treaty of Greenwich with Scotland, which ostensibly gave him the marriage agreement which he wanted, and postponed his commitment against France until the following year. The Emperor, understandably, was not pleased, and before the end of the year the treaty of Greenwich had unravelled. The Scottish regent, the Earl of Arran, defected to the pro-French party, and no amount of military posturing by the English could alter the fact that the effects of Solway Moss had been neutralised, and that the danger of some intervention on the French side in the forthcoming war had actually increased. Meanwhile Lisle was friendly with the Parrs, and Catherine's promotion to the royal bed was good news for him. In January 1544 Eustace Chapuys, the Imperial ambassador, thought him to be one of Henry's closest and most confidential councillors. As the year advanced, it became apparent that another strike northwards would have to precede the French campaign to which the king was irrevocably committed. Lisle was consequently preparing for action on two fronts, and the maritime resources of the country were stretched. At the end of April the Earl of Hertford led 12,000 men on what was really a glorified raid into Scotland, taking and sacking Edinburgh and Leith. Lisle commanded the supporting fleet of about seventy ships, but only eleven of them were royal warships, a quarter of the available fleet, and reflecting the divided priorities of the admiralty. In spite of its lack of real achievement, this violent gesture proved to be sufficient for Henry's immediate purpose, although it did nothing to resurrect the treaty of Greenwich. When the king transported his army royal to France in June, there was no intervention from the north. As the French made no attempt to intercept this invasion the Lord Admiral's role was purely logistic. Although the king accompanied his army in person, the field command was shared between the Dukes of Norfolk and Suffolk. The military honours of the year were thus divided evenly between the two court parties, each of which was required to display the same loyalty and commitment.

The campaign was a mess, and in September a disgruntled Emperor made a separate peace, but it did result in the capture of Boulogne, to Henry's disproportionate delight. When he returned to England he appointed Lord Lisle, who had so far seen very little action, to be Captain of the town, and Senechal of the Boulonnais.[11] Lisle was less than delighted by this evidence of his master's confidence, fearing that he might lose the Admiralty, by which he clearly set great store. However Henry had no such intention, and after a somewhat troubled sojourn of about four months, the Lord Admiral was recalled to go about his proper business of mobilising the fleet for the new campaigning season. 1545 promised to be a very dangerous year, because the English now had no allies, and war on two fronts. However, the threatened French intervention in the north did not materialise, and the Scots proved to be no more than an intermittent nuisance. The real danger lay in Francis's determination to recover Boulogne and to punish Henry for the humiliation of the previous year. By the beginning of June a fleet which may have numbered as many as 300 sail was mobilising in the Seine estuary, and Lisle determined upon a pre-emptive strike. On or about the 25th he endeavoured to enter the Seine with 160 ships and 12,000 men. The weather frustrated him, and all that he accomplished was a successful skirmish with some French galleys off Alderney, but he had for the first time demonstrated his capacity for a large scale command at sea, and ensured that England had mobilised an adequate fleet to meet the impending threat. The French Admiral, d'Annebaut, had to improvise his tactics because he was ready well in advance of the army which was to attack Boulogne, and he could not afford to keep his ships idle. Consequently on the 10th of July he moved against Portsmouth and the Isle of Wight. It is not certain whether he intended to seize the island, or merely to carry out a destructive raid. Whatever his intention, it remained unrealised, because the English were ready for him. His landing parties on the Isle of Wight were repulsed, and Lord Lisle confronted him in the Solent with over 200 ships. No battle ensued, partly because of the fickle winds, and partly because d'Annebaut, mindful of his main mission against Boulogne, backed off rather than face an equal contest. English relief was tempered by the loss of the *Mary Rose*, which went down in a freak accident, taking some 500 men with her, but they had achieved an almost bloodless victory. No one expected this non-event to be decisive, but so it proved. D'Annebaut proceeded to Boulogne, where he landed 7000 men, and then returned to the Sussex coast. Lisle, with about 70 ships, went in pursuit, intending to bring the French to battle. The two fleets encountered on August 15th, and exchanged gunfire, but again the French backed off under cover of darkness, leaving Lisle ascendant but frustrated. It subsequently transpired that plague had broken out in d'Annebaut's fleet, and he was forced to return home and demobilise.

Towards the end of 1545 the Lord Admiral's stock was high. When the Duke of Suffolk died in August, at least one observer believed that his unique place in the king's favour would be inherited by Lord Lisle.[12] That did not happen, and neither did Lisle receive any further important preferments during Henry's lifetime, but he did receive several annuities, and substantial grants of former monastic land, as well as some valuable trading concessions. Nor did he always wait for favours to be bestowed. Like most successful courtiers, he petitioned constantly for grants and concessions, sometimes directly and sometimes using his friend Sir William Paget as an intermediary. Although Paget's favour was no higher than his own, as the king's secretary he had more regular and guaranteed access, particularly when Lisle was away from court discharging his various duties. When the 1545 subsidy was assessed early in the following year his lands were rated at £1376 per annum, probably below their true value, but still making him the eighth or ninth richest peer in England, worth more than several Earls. In spite of this he seems to have felt himself undervalued, and spoke of his lack of 'estimacion'. By this he may have meant a lack of rank, or his failure to secure any position of honour at court; or it may have reflected an awareness of the fact that his vigorous exploitation of a fluid land market had left him without any power base in the country. If that was his meaning, he did nothing to remedy the situation during the remaining seven years of his life.

By the spring of 1546 the king's health was giving cause for serious concern. Henry started off the year as bellicose as ever and Lisle was warned to be ready to command another great fleet during the ensuing summer, but by the end of March the king had changed his mind. Perhaps he was aware that Francis was just as old and weary as himself, or perhaps he was listening at last to those who were telling him that his resources were exhausted. By the middle of April he had decided to negotiate, and named Lisle and Paget as his two principal commissioners. The discussions were fraught with alarms and excursions, but both sides had a will to peace, and by early June agreement had been reached, Henry was to keep Boulogne for eight years, at the end of which time the French would redeem it for 2 million crowns a sum which might well turn out to be beyond them. Scotland was not included, but the English undertook to abstain from further aggression. In the circumstances it was as good a treaty as could have been hoped for, and it was very much Lord Lisle's personal achievement. He had established with d'Annebaut a relationship of trust and mutual respect which materially assisted the negotiation, and made him *persona grata* in France, a fact which was suitably recognised when he was sent across to receive Francis's personal ratification later in the summer. His own king's satisfaction was reflected in the substantial grant of the dissolved hospital of St. John at Clerkenwell, and in the fact that he was one of the sixteen Privy Councillors selected to be an executor of the king's will. Thanks partly to these successes, partly to the political skill of the Earl of Hertford, and partly to the personal influence of Queen Catherine and Sir Anthony Denny, by the end of the year the reforming party enjoyed a complete ascendancy. In July the conservatives had made a last ditch attempt to discredit the queen, and failed. Shortly after the bishop of Winchester committed some venial indiscretion which his enemies were able to exploit to deprive him of the king's increasingly volatile favour, and in November the fatal arrogance of the Earl of Surrey brought a temporary end to the great house of Howard. In January 1547 the Duke of Norfolk and his son were both attainted of high treason, and the Earl was executed. When Henry died on the 28th January, Hertford, Lisle and Paget were the three most powerful men in England, and apparently firm friends as well as allies. The only shadow to darken these successful years in John Dudley's life had been the death of his highly promising eldest son, Henry, in 1544. Henry had joined his father at Boulogne, and been knighted by the king at the end of September. A few weeks late he died at the age of nineteen, a victim of sickness rather than war, but so sparse is the documentation of Dudley's private life that we have no idea how either he or his wife responded to the tragedy. He may have reflected philosophically that he had been blessed with five other sons. Such a powerful vein of good fortune could stand a few setbacks.

VI Earl of Warwick, 1547-1549

Edward VI was nine and half years old when his father died, and the collective responsibility apparently envisaged in Henry's will did not provide a viable form of Regency government. Consequently the first action of his executors when they assembled at the Tower of London on the 31st January was to create the two offices of Lord Protector of the Realm and Governor of the King's person, and to bestow both upon the Earl of Hertford.13 In return he was bound to govern with their advice and consent. They then constituted themselves into the Privy Council of King Edward VI, and obtained the young king's formal ratification of what they had done. If there were any dissenting voices among the executors at this stage, they did not succeed in recording their presence. A few days later, on the 6th February, they addressed themselves to what might be described as the fruits of victory. Henry had undoubtedly intended some 'replenishment' of the peerage, and other rewards and promotions, in the last weeks of his life. There is plenty of independent testimony to that fact. But whether he intended what now emerged is more open to question. On the 17th February, the day after Henry's funeral, the Earl of Hertford became Duke of Somerset, Thomas Wriothesley the Lord Chancellor became Earl of Southampton, William Parr, Earl of Essex, became Marquis of Northampton, and Viscount Lisle became Earl of Warwick. Four baronies were also bestowed, one of them upon the Protector's younger brother, Thomas, who had been sworn of the Privy Council shortly before Henry's death, and was an assistant executor. At the same time the Duke of Somerset assumed the office of Lord Treasurer, vacated by the fall of the Duke of Norfolk, the Earl of Warwick became Lord Great Chamberlain. and Lord Thomas Seymour became Lord Admiral. How pleased John Dudley was with these arrangements, and whether he had been consulted about them, we do not know.

As we have seen, Dudley had hankered after 'estimacion' for several years. Now he had an Earldom and a great court office; he was also recognised as one of the most powerful men in England. On the other hand he had lost the Admiralty, and now held no office of state. There are some hints that he was not pleased by that development, and it was later alleged that he encouraged the disaffection of the one man who was really offended by the allocations of February 1547, the Protector's brother, Thomas Seymour. Seymour was deeply affronted first by the fact that both the Protectorship and the Governorship had been conferred on his brother; and secondly by the fact that Edward became a Duke, while he received only a barony.

He grumbled to his friends that he was equally the king's uncle, and should have received at least the Governorship, but whether the Earl of Warwick encouraged him in that ambition remains an open question. At the time of Seymour's fall early in 1549 Warwick claimed that he had exerted himself to heal the rift between the brothers, and had encouraged the Admiral to accept his 'honourable estate'.**14** The case against the Earl really depends upon hindsight, and there are no other suggestions that he was undermining the Protector's position in 1547. Warwick was one of the half dozen or so councillors who attended every meeting between the 29th January and the 12th March, and certainly supported the Protector over the dismissal of Lord Chancellor Wriothesley on the 5th March. Wriothesley was the only powerful conservative to have survived in favour at the end of Henry's reign. There is no evidence that he had opposed the creation of the Protectorate. He may have been seen as an obstacle to Somerset's intended religious policy, but the real reason for his removal was almost certainly his opposition to the extension of the Protector's powers, which was under discussion during February. Wriothesley may have been guilty of a technical infringement when he put the judicial aspect of his office into commission. If so, it was a genuine mistake, and warranted no more than a reproof; his dismissal was a political coup. On the 12th March Somerset received a patent under the Great Seal, granting him full regency powers until the king came of age, including the power to appoint and dismiss Privy Councillors. In the middle of February the Imperial ambassador, Francois Van der Delft, predicted a rift between Somerset and Warwick, on the grounds that both were ambitious and that Warwick was the more popular. However he retracted this opinion some time before a real rift appeared, and early in 1549 described Warwick as well satisfied with the position which he had achieved. He also described Wriothesley as one of the most powerful members of the council just a few days before his fall, so the accuracy of his observation is open to serious doubt.

Early in March Warwick was commissioned, along with Paget, to complete the work which they had carried out in 1546 by settling the boundaries of the Boulogne Pale. This they did successfully, but the death of Francis I at the beginning of April nullified their efforts. Henry II refused to ratify the draft agreement, and the English council expected an early return to war. However, as the summer advanced and French hostility continued to be confined to words, the Protector decided to proceed with the uncompleted business which he had inherited in Scotland. Preparations for this campaign probably account for the absence of the Earl of Warwick from the council during most of the summer. There is little surviving evidence of his activity during these months, except for his pursuit of a substantial grant of land from the Court of Augmentations. He was due to receive an additional estate to the value of £300 per annum under the terms of his patent of creation, and had clearly been allowed to put in his own bid. After consultation with Paget, who was still close to both Warwick and the Protector, he put in a petition running to 29 membranes, asking particularly for the lordship of Warwick '...because of the name and my descent from one of the daughters of the lawful line'. On the 22nd of June he received his grant, which differed in many respects from the petition, but which included the lordship of Warwick.**15**

The Earl's power strategy at this point, if he had one, is not very obvious. In spite of his eagerness to obtain Warwick, there is little sign of an attempt to build a power base in the West Midlands. Much of the land which he received by this grant he sold again within a few months, and his involvement with the market generally continued to be large, suggesting a policy of trading for profit, and possibly brokering, rather than an ambition for regional domination. On the other hand the names of his customers, or at least some of them, were those of men with whom he already had, or was endeavouring to build, a political relationship; Sir Edward North, Sir Thomas Palmer, Sir Thomas Darcy, Francis Jobson and George Harper. It therefore looks as though he was using land, not granted in the ancient manner but sold at favourable rates, in order to build an affinity. The fact that these men, like the lands themselves, were scattered all over the country, confirms that his ambition was national rather than local, but it would be unwise to read too much into such fragmentary evidence. Some eight or nine members of the House of Commons elected in the autumn of 1547 can also be identified as friends or dependents of Warwick's, but there is no evidence at all to suggest that he obtained, or even sought, their election. His gains also need to be kept in proportion. On the 9th July 1547 the Protector received an annuity of 8000 marks (£5,333), and on the 19th August Lord Thomas Seymour was granted an additional estate worth £500 a year.

 In August Somerset put the country on a war footing. This was an unusual arrangement, but the circumstances were unusual as there had not been a working minority government since the 1430s. The Protector appointed himself 'King's Lieutenant and Captain General for the wars...', with the Earl of Warwick as Lieutenant
and Captain General of the North and Lord Thomas Seymour, the Lord Admiral, for the South. By this time there was virtually no Anglophile party in Scotland, although the protestants who were beginning to appear naturally tended to

be anti-French. During the previous year a protestant commando had succeeded in assassinating the leader of the French party, Cardinal David Beaton, and had seized St. Andrews castle. At the end of July 1547, as though to demonstrate the worthlessness of English support, a French fleet bombarded the castle into submission and carried off the garrison as prisoners. Henry II, however, was a little too contemptuous of the English. He had other things to do, and did not bother to send any troops to the north, in spite of the obvious signs of military preparations south of the border. Consequently when the Protector crossed the Tweed with 18,000 men on the 2nd September, the Scots who confronted him were on their own. The Earl of Warwick commanded the vanguard, and Lord Clinton the supporting fleet since the Lord Admiral remained on his charge in the south of England. The campaign which followed was swift and effective. Three years later, when circumstances had changed dramatically, Warwick was to claim the chief credit for this, but it is clear from contemporary accounts that the main strategy and command were Somerset's. Warwick was a dashing and enterprising cavalry commander, who in spite of his advancing years could still distinguish himself in personal combat, but his responsibility was simply that of a senior field officer. The two armies met on the 10th September at Pinkie Cleugh, near the crossing of the Esk. Unlike Solway Moss, this was a hard fought battle, and the casualties were heavy, but the result was the same, a decisive English victory.

    Having razed Leith, and reduced the Scots for the time being to a condition of military helplessness, the English retreated and Somerset returned immediately to London. There had been some ominous rumours that his brother's responsibilities had gone to his head, and he was boasting that he would shortly be made a duke. Warwick remained in the north, along with Sir Ralph Sadler, to negotiate with the commissioners whom the Scottish Regent had undertaken to send to discuss terms. The commissioners never came, and at some point before the end of November, Warwick returned to London. He is not noted as being present at the parliament which convened on the 4th November, and does not seem to have been attending council meetings. The first record of his presence in the south is a letter dated from Ely place on the 8th January 1548, but he was almost certainly at court over Christmas. On the 22nd December he received a further land grant worth £108 a year for his services in Scotland; considerably less, it may be noted, than the Protector awarded himself. On the 24th December Somerset had his patent of appointment renewed and extended '...for as much as by his (the king's) said uncle and council affairs have been well managed...'. Warwick did not set his hand to this instrument, but that is of no significance since it was confirmed by the king in person. There is no sign of a rift between the two at this point, and Warwick was approached by a number of petitioners who continued to regard him as one of the Protector's most influential friends. Odet de Selve, the French ambassador, also commented upon the close relationship existing between the two men. One of the reasons for Warwick's prolonged absence from the council may have been poor health. He seems to have been frequently indisposed, and complained of ailments which sound to the modern ear like colds and indigestion. Both Van der Delft and de Selve commented upon this proclivity, but since neither his mental nor his physical energy seem to have been impaired, both hypochondria and dissimulation are possible. As the council was being increasingly marginalised by the Protector during 1548, Warwick may have regarded attendance as a waste of time, and concentrated upon keeping his direct lines of communication with Somerset in good repair. At some point during June he was appointed President of the Council in the Marches of Wales. There is no trace of his commission, either in the council register or on the patent roll, but he held the office for about eighteen months. He took it with some reluctance, protesting that he did not have enough status in the borders, which is an interesting comment, considering that his principal seat was in Worcestershire, and that he held extensive lands in that county, in Shropshire and in Staffordshire. He was well enough aware that land ownership alone did not create *manred*. As far as can be discovered he never visited Ludlow, or presided over the council in person. Nevertheless, one of the few records of his activity as President discloses a vulnerable streak in his personality. Somerset had assured him of support in making some changes to the council which Warwick had considered to be necessary, but he had failed to remove an (unnamed) judge whom he considered to be corrupt, and he complained bitterly to William Cecil 'By whose persuasion this happens., I know not, but I am sure I have base friends who smile to see me so used...who have now won their purpose, not the first or last to be worked with my lord(16).

In spite of the power and wealth which he had achieved, he still suffered from an insecurity which made him liable to petty out bursts of this kind. Some aspects of his subsequent behaviour can possibly be explained in these terms.

Although he continued to use the good offices of Paget when he was absent from the court, he was less close to his former ally by the end of 1548, and had started to confide in William Cecil, who was the Protector's secretary. Warwick at this point still regarded his relationship with the Protector as the key to power, and assiduously maintained good relations, not only with Cecil, but also with Sir John Thynne and other of the Duke's dependents. There was plague in London during the summer, and the Earl's whereabouts are unknown, but he was back at Ely Place by September, and was present at the second parliamentary session of the reign, which convened on the 27th November. This was the session which passed the first Act of Uniformity, and drew together the threads of the Protector's policy of gradual protestant conversion. Warwick had from the start been an active supporter of that policy, and Van der Delft had noted with disapproval as early as December 1547 that mass was no longer celebrated in his household. He made several recorded interventions during the debate on the bill of uniformity in the House of Lords. They show no understanding of the theological issues under discussion, and an ill-concealed impatience with episcopal disagreements and uncertainties. The bill seems to have been given a much rougher passage in the Lords than in the Commons, and it was important that it should pass, but the Earl of Warwick seems to have had little use for the arts of persuasion.

 1548 was another active year of land dealing, but there was no noticeable rise in his income. Indeed a subsidy assessment of this year shows him worth £1200 a year in lands. The absolute decline from 1546 need not be taken seriously, because assessments were already beginning to lose touch with reality, but the number of peers rated above him. was significantly larger than two years before. Either Warwick enjoyed an position which enabled him to obtain an especially favourable assessment, or he was losing out in the competition for grants and needed to take remedial action. During July 1548 he also had a significant clash with John Hales the agrarian reformer. Hales was very pro-active in Somerset's campaign to put teeth into the traditional Tudor policy of curbing enclosure. The enclosure of arable land, and its subsequent conversion to sheep farming, was widely believed to be the root of agrarian unemployment and widespread social discontent. Modern economic analysis suggests that this was a mistaken view, but it was held at the time with the fervour of a moral crusade. Somerset endeavoured to approach this problem by establishing commissions of enquiry, one of which, in the West Midland, was led by Hales. Warwick took the view that these commissions, strongly tinged as they were with class resentment against the gentry and aristocracy, were subversive of good order, and were encouraging the commons to take the law into their own hands. Historians from John Strype to R.H. Tawney have given John Dudley a roasting for this unsympathetic and authoritarian reaction, but the severe disturbances of 1549, and his own subsequent success in keeping the lid on a turbulent situation indicate that he was probably right.

By the end of 1548 the Protector was in severe difficulties. His policy of establishing English garrisons to control the lowlands of Scotland had been an expensive failure. On the 15th June 6000 French troops had landed at Leith, and less than a month later the Scots had renewed the auld alliance and betrothed their infant queen to the dauphin. In the middle of August Mary departed for France. The treaty of Greenwich was dead and buried, and Somerset's whole strategy since the battle of Pinkie had collapsed. To make matters worse, instead of accepting this defeat, and waiting for the vicissitudes of Scottish politics to restore an English advantage, he reverted to a policy of claiming suzerainty over the northern kingdom, and thereby discredited what had appeared to be an enlightened attempt at unification. At the same time the behaviour of his brother Lord Thomas Seymour had become intolerable. Having first affronted the Protector by a secret marriage to the Queen Dowager, Catherine Parr, in the spring of 1547, he had then quarrelled bitterly with his brother over Catherine's jewels, and taken advantage of Somerset's lax control of the Privy Chamber to ingratiate himself with the young king. This he had done by feeding him sums of money via John Fowler, one of the Grooms.[17] When Catherine died in childbirth in September 1548, Seymour began to intrigue recklessly for the hand of the fifteen year old Princess Elizabeth. He seems to have been a man incapable of distinguishing between political reality and his own ambitious fantasies. One of the games which he played was to calculate the power of an imaginary affinity, with which he seems to have believed that he could defy the Protector and his allies. Another was to mobilise a party in the House of Lords and have his brother's patent annulled by statute. He discovered that Sir William Sharrington, the Treasurer of the Bristol mint, was fiddling the books, and blackmailed him out of considerable sums, which he seems to have spent on equipment for his largely non-existent followers. It is difficult to see that Seymour in himself constituted any real threat, but his extravagant language attracted the attention of both the French and Imperial ambassadors, who began to wonder whether they could use him for their masters' purposes. Eventually the beleaguered Somerset lost patience with his brother. In January 1549 he was arrested and interrogated. Under questioning he denied any treasonable intent but refused to give specific answers, which made the whole business of disentangling fact from fantasy impossible. Perhaps for that reason he was not tried but convicted by Act of Attainder and executed in March.

    John Heyward, writing in the early seventeenth century, attributed Seymour's downfall to a machiavellian intrigue on the part of the Earl of Warwick. Warwick, so the argument runs, deliberately encouraged Seymour's pretensions in order to create a rift between the brothers, which he could then use to discredit the Protector. By the time that Hayward was writing, this view was conventional wisdom because of the 'black legend' created by Warwick's eventual fate, but it is unsupported by contemporary evidence. Whether or not he had made the efforts which he claimed to reconcile the brothers, by late 1548 Seymour clearly regarded him as an ally of the Protector, and an opponent of his own designs. Nor does it appear that Somerset was much weakened at the time by his handling of the issue. After his fall it was easy enough to add parracide to the charges against him, but in the early weeks of 1549 the council shared his concern and alarm to the full, and even excused him from attendance in the Lords while the attainder was under consideration. Seymour clearly had all the charm which often accompanies complete irresponsibility, and in other circumstances might have been no more than an amiable and harmless rogue, but as Lord Admiral and a person close to the centre of power, his behaviour was totally unacceptable.

Apart from dealing with his brother, Somerset had two other preoccupations in the early weeks of 1549, and neither of them reflect any credit on his judgement. He was preparing a new large-scale campaign against Scotland, and he was determined to press ahead with the enclosure commissions. In the spring, Warwick was ill again, but he was back at court by the end of May, when he was appointed General of the army against Scotland. Whether he ever set out for the north is a matter of some doubt, because by the end of June the domestic situation was giving rise to serious concern. In early July Warwick was at Ely Place, urging Sir John Thynne to convince the Protector of the need for tough action. He was not even sure, he claimed, that he could trust his own men to hold Warwick castle.18 However, if, he held Somerset to blame for this situation, he gave no sign of it at that stage. It was not a time for the council to display disunity. For the time being Somerset confined himself to issuing proclamations denouncing the commons for taking the law into their own hands, and urging the magistrates to do their duty. It was not until August, when such measures had clearly failed that he finally abandoned the campaign in Scotland, and recalled troops which had been mustered to deal with the mounting crisis East Anglia, the Midlands and the South West.

VII The Reins of Power, 1549-1550

About fifteen counties were affected by disturbances of varying severity. In some, such as Wiltshire, determined or well organised gentry quickly had the situation under control; in others, such as Suffolk and Sussex, the rioters were 'appeased...by fair persuasions...' The most intractable problems were presented by counties which had no clear local leadership. This was true to some extent in Oxfordshire, but most notably in Norfolk, Devon and Cornwall. In Norfolk the fall of the Howards had left a political vaccuum, because although the bulk of the Duke's estates had passed to the Princess Mary she was either unable, or unwilling, to offer any leadership in this crisis. In the south west the destruction of the Courtenays had created a similar problem. Lord John Russell held most of the Marquis of Exeter's lands, but he was non-resident and commanded no traditional respect. The grievances of the protesters were not everywhere the same. In the midlands conventional enclosure featured largely, and the riots were most closely associated with the commissions of enquiry. In East Anglia encroachment on common land was a more emotive issue, and the leaders were substantial yeomen. In the South West the Prayer Book, introduced at Whitsun, had detonated a range of grievances, both secular and religious, but the leading role played by the clergy has always caused this to be known as the 'prayer book rebellion'. For several weeks in the face of this conflagration, the Protector temporised, unwilling to admit that he could have been even partly responsible for stirring up such a hornets' nest. He was also desperately short of resources until the troops recalled from the north, including several bands of mercenaries, could be re-deployed. The Earl of Warwick remained in London, where during July he busied himself about the defence of the city, and of Windsor castle. Somerset seems to have intended to send him to the south west, but in the event Russell, Grey and Herbert were sent instead. By the end of the month he had probably grasped his own personal nettle, and gone down to Warwick to rally the gentlemen of the West Midlands. He was certainly in Warwick on the 10th August, when he was summoned to cope with a different emergency. The Protector himself seems to have found it necessary to stay at Westminster, and towards the end of July committed a campaign against the Norfolk rebels to the innocuous William Parr, Marquis of Northampton. The great camp on Mousehold heath, more than any of the other disturbances, had managed to retain the face of peaceful protest, but it had proved impossible to dissolve by peaceful means, and could not be ignored. Parr, who had no military experience, advanced incautiously with insufficient force, and was repulsed from the city of Norwich with some loss. Robert Kett, the rebel leader, had no idea how to exploit his victory, and the set back was more an embarrassment than a danger, but Somerset could not afford to make a second mistake, and therefore summoned his companion in arms John Dudley to put the situation right.

Warwick moved swiftly, but methodically. The demoralised East Anglian gentry were summoned to meet him at Cambridge on the 15th August with such men as they could raise. Meanwhile he summoned his own followers and took over the command of about 1400 seasoned mercenaries, mostly German and Italian. Altogether his force numbered about 6000 infantry and 1500 cavalry, more than twice that which Northampton had deployed. He had no intention of risking a similar rebuff. On the 23rd August, having reached Intwood, two miles from the rebel camp, he offered pardon in return for immediate surrender. Kett might have been prepared to consider such an offer, realising that the odds were now against him, but his men were recalcitrant, and left him with no option but to fight it out. The following night Warwick moved a part of his infantry against the rebel held city, and Kett's men were driven out after fierce street fighting. Forty nine prisoners were hanged in the market place on the Earl's orders. Two days later, being now cut off from all supplies, Kett was forced to abandon his fortified camp, and risk the chances of open battle. He probably still had a considerable numerical advantage, as the camp had contained over 12,000 men at its peak, but neither he nor anyone with him had military experience. The battle of 'Dussindale' which followed was not so much a fight as a rout and slaughter, in which at least 2000 of the rebels perished. The campaign probably cost about 3000 lives on both sides, because the royal army also suffered losses, but Warwick's victory had been complete. Unlike Russell in the south west, he then restrained the gentlemen's desire for vengeance, and the number of executions which followed was limited to a few dozen. 'There must be measure kept, and above all things in punishment men must not exceed', he is alleged to have said. He got little thanks from those he had spared, and remained for years the most hated man in Norfolk.

When he returned to London at the end of August, a crisis was clearly brewing. It was claimed by one who was an eyewitness, but writing many years after the event, that during his campaign in East Anglia, Warwick was bitterly critical of the Protector, blaming his policies for the unnecessary shedding of English blood.19 There is no contemporary confirmation of this, and the evidence suggests that relations between the two men had remained friendly, at least until some point during the summer. Warwick's chatty correspondence with Sir John Thynne came to an end during July, and that may have some significance. On the 9th of August Henry II, sensing the opportunity created by the English disorders, declared war, and the Emperor had already announced categorically that he would offer no support for the defence of Boulogne. Somerset's policies appeared to be failing in every direction, and he was becoming increasingly isolated. Order had been restored, but the credit had gone to Russell, Grey and Warwick rather than the Protector, and the situation remained extremely tense. For the time being Boulogne was holding out, but most of the Boullonais had been overrun, and the last important English garrison in Scotland, Haddington, had been abandoned. Sir William Paget, originally Somerset's right hand man, had seen trouble coming over a year earlier, as the Protector became increasingly autocratic and unwilling to listen to advice. His warnings had become steadily more urgent and explicit, but seem to have passed unheeded. Given the circumstances of a royal minority, the hostility of Henry II and the uncertain friendship of Charles V, the last thing England needed was internal dissension, and yet the Protector had embarked upon not just one controversial policy, but two. While he was alienating the aristocracy by insisting upon his vision of social justice, he was also splitting the country down the middle by his religious reforms. How much longer could the country go on debilitating itself in this manner?

We do not know who originally decided that Somerset must go, and it may well not have been one individual. On the 15th September Van der Delft reported that the Protector had a scheme for the formation of a 'new council', and that this was provoking strong opposition from several nembers of the existing council. Just what this scheme may have been was not explained, and it may never have existed. What is important is that he named the principal objectors as the Earls of Arundel, Southampton and Warwick, and identified the source of his information as the Princess Mary.[20] Mary had told the ambassador that she had been approached by the Earls, who had canvassed her support for the Protector's overthrow, but that she had disclaimed any wish to be involved. Had she been willing, it is probable that they would have offered her the regency, but no such offer is mentioned as having been made at this point. Van der Delft then received a visit from Paget, who solicited his assistance in bringing Warwick to '...a better disposition regarding religion'. This cryptic request can only have meant 'to influence him in a conservative direction.' Arundel, Wriothesley, and other probable conspiritors, such as Lord St. John, were all know conservatives. So Paget, who knew which way the wind was blowing, was trying to avoid a split among the conspiritors on religious lines. The ambassador was then visited, at some point before 23rd September, by Warwick himself. The Earl was not seeking the spiritual guidance which Paget thought he needed, but making clear his extreme dissatisfaction with Somerset's government, and hinting obliquely at a reversal of the Protector's religious policy and a rapprochement with the Emperor. It does not necessarily follow from this that Warwick was the original ringleader, or even that he was the leader at this point, but it does prove that he was a committed member of the group, and not a belated or reluctant recruit. His motivation can only be re-constructed. He displayed some personal animus against the Duchess of Somerset but not against the Duke, and there is no evidence that his political hostility went back before the summer of 1549. Religion was not high among his priorities, and we should probably conclude that he saw himself as acting dispassionately in the public interest. His leading role was not so much due to thrusting ambition as to his natural status among his peers, and the fact that he had brought a sizeable military force back with him from Norfolk.

Because of this, and because of the prestige of his victory over Kett, Warwick had a high profile at the end of September. He also had useful friends in the City of London, and it was there that the conspiritors began to gather in the early days of October. Somerset either did not see, or did not chose to heed, the signs of trouble ahead. The only sign that he had observed the stealthy mobilisation which was going on was a proclamation dated 30th September, ordering all soldiers to leave the city and return to their places of duty. As Richard Grafton put it '..many of the Lordes of the Realme, as well counsaylors as others myslykyng the gouvernement of the Protector, began to withdrawe themselves from the Courte...'[21]

By the 5th October the king was at Hampton Court, with Somerset, Paget, and the two secretaries, Petre and Smith. The remainder of the council, with a handful of exceptions, were in

London. Apart from the king's guard, numbering at most 200, and a similar number of his own men, the Protector had no force at his disposal. How many men the conspiritors had is not clear, but far more, perhaps as many as 2500. However Lords Russell and Grey were returning slowly from the south west with at least as many again, having ignored orders to disband. Both sides solicited their assistance. Realising that the odds were swiftly piling up against him, on the 5th October Somerset issued a general summons to all the king's loyal subjects to muster at Hampton Court to defend his royal person against a most dangerous and subversive conspiracy. It was a fatal mistake. The only person of any importance who joined him was archbishop Cranmer, with 60 men. The hundreds of unarmed or half armed peasants who began to assemble aroused most painful memories of the early summer, and alarmed Somerset's friends far more than they did his enemies. Hampton Court was not defensible with the kind of force he was likely to have, and on the evening of the 6th October, the Protector decamped to Windsor Castle, taking the king with him. He had now painted himself into a corner. Russell and Grey rejected his overtures, citing their specific unhappiness with his 'raising of the commons'; and the move to Windsor could easily be made to look like a kidnapping. By the 7th October the 'London Lords' held all the cards - except the king. Not only did Edward's presence at Windsor inhibit any attempt at a military solution, it also meant that Somerset could still issue authentic royal commands, which the Lords could not.

    This deadlock was eventually broken in a series of letters and messages exchanged on the 7th and 8th October between the council on the one hand, and Somerset, Paget and Cranmer on the other, using Sir Philip Hoby, who was thought to enjoy the confidence of both sides, as a go-between. Those letters which survive only partly explain the outcome, because they were mostly preserved by the council in order to justify its position. Significantly, on the 8th, Somerset appealed directly to his former friendship with the Earl of Warwick '...for the love that hath ever been betwixt us or that hereafter may be, persuade yourself with truth, and let this time declare to me and the world your just honour and perseverence in friendship...*22*

How Warwick responded, if at all, we do not know, but it is clear that certain critical elements in the exchange were never recorded. The breakthrough came on the 10th October when the Protector surrendered by allowing himself to be dismissed from the royal presence, and permitting his servants to be replaced by the king's own men. He had already told Cranmer that he set no store by his office, believing that he had been called to it by the council, but that he would not stand down unconditionally. We must therefore conclude that his conditions had been met in a secret undertaking, but what they were and who offerred them, can only be surmised. The subsequent course of events, however, suggests that the Earl of Warwick and the archbishop were the key players at this critical stage. Somerset could hardly have demanded less than a guarentee of his life and at least some portion of his fortune, but it must also be remembered that he was a genuine and committed protestant. Cranmer's co-operation would also have had a price, and for him the protection of religious reform had the highest possible priority. As well as being by this time the leader of the council, Warwick was probably the only senior nobleman who would have been able and willing to guarentee the continuation of religious reform. Conservative retrenchment was a price which he would have been willing to pay in order to force Somerset out of office, but whatever his personal preferences may have been, continued reform would offer him the best chance of remaining in charge.

On the 14th of October Somerset was committed to the Tower, and a number of his close associates, including Sir Mchael Stanhope, the Chief Gentleman of the Privy Chamber, were imprisoned along with him. The Privy Chamber was then recontructed to include six noblemen and four principal gentlemen. 23 One of the noblemen was Warwick hinself, and one of the gentlemen his brother Andrew. Of the remaining eight, four could be classed as his allies. However there was at first no sign of factional division among the victors, religious or otherwise, and no power struggle. The council had a conservative majority, and on the 17th October Van der Delft observed that all the lords except the Earl of Warwick were devoted to the old faith. Warwick, he believed, was also moving in the same direction, and the archbishop of Canterbury would soon be removed from office. It is possible that another approach was made to Mary at this point, but if so the Earl of Warwick was not a party to it, and the result was the same as before. The reforming preachers and clergy had feared the worst from the Protector's departure, and continued to hold their breath throughout late October and November. There were rumours that the imprisoned conservative bishops, Stephen Gardiner and Edmund Bonner would be released, but nothing happened. The Imperial ambassador became puzzled, and then suspicious. On the 19th of October Warwick resumed the office of Lord Admiral, but no great significance can be attached to that as the position had been vacant since January, and he was the obvious man to fill it. On the 6th of November a genuine straw appeared on the wind when Thomas Goodrich, the bishop of Ely, was sworn of the council. Goodrich was a protestant, and he was preferred to Sir Thomas Arundel, who was a strong religious conservative, a supporter of Mary and a protege of the Earl of Southampton. One contemporary, although writing several years later, remembered that it was at this time that the Earl of Warwick '...by the means of the archbishop of Canterbury (procured) great friends about the king'. Whatever that may mean, it clearly suggests that the reformers had control over access to Edward, with whose developing religious prejudices they were so much more in tune. The king was twelve by this time, and his personality was emerging strongly. It would be an exaggeration to say that he was influencing policy, but the politically astute believed that his majority was only six years off. Those who intended to survive to influence the mature man would therefore be well advised to pay attention to the wishes of the youth.

As late as the 7th November Van der Delft still believed that Southampton was 'head' of the council, but in fact he had not attended a meeting since the 21st October, and his influence was on the wane. This seems to have been due mainly to a genuine illness, but the fact that his protege Sir Edward Peckham disappeared shortly afterwards meant that the balance in the council was tilting slightly but significantly in Warwick's favour. By late November Dudley was also ill with a 'rume' in the head, but this did not mean that he and Wriothesley were equally hors de combat. When Warwick kept his chamber, the council came to him, whereas Southampton absented himself. This contrast was clearly reflected when the Marquis of Dorset was admitted to the council on the 29th November. Henry Grey was the husband of Frances, nee Brandon, the king's cousin. He was also a protestant, and an ally of Warwick. Although there had been no overt struggle, by the beginning of December the council had been turned around, and now had a majority in favour of continued reformation. Nevertheless, as late as the 5th December Warwick does not seem to have seen himself as the leader of a faction, victorious or otherwise. According to one well informed observer, he was then intending to assume Somerset's former office as Lord Treasurer himself, to hand over his existing office as Lord Great Chamberlain to the Earl of Arundel; and to promote William Paget, recently made a baron, from Controller to Lord Chamberlain.24 However within a few days the whole situation had changed, and the illusion of consensus had been shattered.

What seems to have happened is that William Petre, Lord St. John, previously a fairly pragmatic conservative, sought out the Earl of Warwick and warned him that the Earls of Arundel and Southampton, supported by a few lesser councillors, were planning to use the case then being prepared against the Duke of Somerset as a means of bringing about his overthrow. It was later alleged that the plotters were intending to press for a death sentence against the fallen Protector, and in the process to incriminate Warwick as his accomplice, using the evidence of their earlier friendship. Given the balance of power in the council by early December, this seems far-fetched, and no charges along those lines were ever pressed. If, however, Warwick and Cranmer had given undertakings to Somerset of which most of the council were ignorant, the execution of the latter would have driven a wedge between the Earl and the archbishop, and split the reforming party right down the middle. It was not so much Warwick's life which was threatened as his political ascendency. Armed with St. John's information, on or about the 13th December, he staged a dramatic scene. When the council assembled at Ely place the Earl of Southampton, who had recently returned to the board, '...proposed how worthy the Lord Protector was to die and for how many high treasons'. Whereupon Warwick proclaimed with a vehemence which stunned the meeting that whoever sought the Duke's blood sought his own also. **25** This public rebuff proved decisive, because the conservatives were neither numerous enough no resolute enough to recover from being wrong footed. Lord Russell, like St. John a shrewd opportunist, had already switched to the winning side. Southampton, Arundel and Sir Robert Southwell were caught in the open. Southwell was arrested and dismissed from the council on the 29th December, and the Earls had followed him by the end of January. On the 19th January St. John became Earl of Wiltshire, and on the 3rd February 1550 Lord Treasurer. At the same time Russell became Earl of Bedford. Paget, touched but not incriminated, never obtained the Chamberlainship for which he had been destined, and never recovered Warwick's confidence. Sir Thomas Darcy and Walter Devereux, Lord Ferrers, both protestants, joined council during January. Whether the Arundel/Southampton 'conspiracy' was real, fabricated or merely exaggerated is not entirely clear. What is clear is that it gave the Earl of Warwick an unchallenged political ascendency which he had not enjoyed after the overthrow of the Protector. It was probably not a carefully planned coup but a piece of brilliant opportunism which originated more in an instinct for survival than in ruthless ambition. Whatever it was, it created a new political situation, and introduced the last and most spectacular phase of John Dudley's career.

VIII Lord President of the Council, 1550-1552

No sooner had Warwick declared his position during December than Somerset was offered, and accepted, thirty one articles of submission. The crisis over his fate was ended. A bill for his fine and ransome, which indicated that no criminal charges would be pressed, was introduced into parliament on the 2nd January, and had passed all it stages by the 14th. Meanwhile the public policy of the new regime was beginning to take shape. Parliament had re-convened on the 4th November, and had immediately begun to show a different set of priorities. The traumatic events of the summer quickly produced an act 'for the punishment of unlawful assembles'. Somerset's sheep and cloth tax was repealed and replaced with an ordinary subsidy; and an act 'concerning the improvement of commons and waste grounds' reversed the tendency of recent years by reviving the Statute of Merton and allowing landlords to enclose under certain circumstances. On the 25th December the council issued a proclamation emphasising its support for the Book of Common Prayer, and denouncing those who sought to reintroduce 'vain and superstitious ceremonies' on the grounds that the book had been the work of the fallen Protector.26 Whether by accident or design, by February 1550 the Earl of Warwick found himself bearing the principal responsibility for an extremely beleaguered regime. Apart from the potentiality for religious strife, there was the prospect of another tense and dangerous summer in the countryside, war with both France and Scotland, and a mounting financial crisis of truly alarming proportions. Failure to resolve all or any of these problems would at least ruin his chances of retaining the king's confidence past his eighteenth birthday, and might result in his immediate and violent overthrow.

In these difficult circumstances his main strategy was simple and effective; to concentrate upon the political education of the king, and to ease him gradually into an effective operational role. This necessitated the abandonment of the discredited office of Protector, with its overt image of regency, and resort to a certain amount of subterfuge. Edward continued to receive a conventional education. He became highly proficient in latin, and was deeply interested in theology. But he was also encouraged to write political and administrative papers; what would now be called 'problem solving' exercises. This was sometimes done directly, and sometimes indirectly via William Thonas, a clerk of the Privy Council who sent him, ostensibly on his own initiative, a series of papers on the nature of monarchy, and on financial matters. Thomas adopted a conspiritorial air, suggesting that, with a little help from his friends, the boy would be able to amaze his seasoned councillors with his grasp of affairs. In effect Edward was being invited to act the part of the king which he would shortly become. Psychologically this was a very good strategy. Not only did it give the boy, who was highly intelligent, a precocious grasp of affairs, it also gave him a profound respect and liking for the Earl of Warwick. Because this education was cut off by sickness and death before it could be completed, we do not know whether it would have worked. It also left behind a puzzle. To what extent during the last eighteen months of Edward's life, did the act become a reality? Probably even those who were closest to him did not quite know. Somerset had started by dealing with a child, and his failure to appreciate the fact that children grow up contributed to his downfall. By 1549 Edward had been quite old enough to resent being treated like a piece of fragile luggage. Warwick, on the other hand, knew that he was dealing with an adolescent who would shortly become a very powerful man. That knowledge influenced his public policy in a number of important ways.

This was most obviously the case over religion. Warwick's willingness to go along with the programme launched by

Cranmer and the Protector was influenced by short term tactical considerations, but it was also consistent with the reforming sympathies which he had been exhibiting for some time. However, his decision to throw his weight behind the more radical programme being promoted after 1550 by John Hooper, John Knox and John Harley cannot be explained in the same way. It led to a steady cooling in his relationship with the archbishop, and with Nicholas Ridley, the highly competent and forceful bishop of London. As President of the Council after February 1550 he pushed for Hooper's elevation to the see of Worcester, which was eventually accomplished after much skirmishing with that prickly idealogue in March 1551. In October 1552 he was pressing for the promotion of Knox to Rochester, on the ground that he would 'quicken' the archbishop of Canterbury, 'whereof he hath need'. That he did not accomplish, but chiefly, it would seem on account of his own disillusionment with the pugnacious Scot. This course of action could be explained by assuming that Warwick had been converted to radical theology, and had become 'an intrepid soldier of Christ', as Hooper called him at one point. The evidence against this is circumstantial but telling. Not only did he renounce protestantism entirely after his fall in 1553, but he was already suspected of being a 'carnal gospeller' by genuine radicals a year earlier. His quarrel with Knox is alleged to have come about because the latter denounced him to his face as a dissembler. Warwick's radicalism was tactical and political, for two very good reasons. In the first place the radicals supported a policy of further disendowing the church. They were not opposed to episcopacy as such, but they believed that bishops should be 'unlorded', and converted into preachers and pastoral supervisors. This was very convenient for a council which had recently confiscated the property of all intercessory foundations on the grounds that they were 'superstitious', and had thereby acquired a capital asset of some £600,000. Warwick forced a number of bishops into unfavourable exchanges with the Crown, reducing the value of some sees, such as Exeter, by as much as 40%. On the appointment of the radical John Ponet to the see of Winchester in 1551, the whole endowment was retained in the king's hands, and Ponet was paid a salary of 2000 marks per annum, less than half the ancient income of the see. Towards the end of 1552 it was proposed to dissolve the diocese of Durham (the second richest in England), and to replace it with two very modestly endowed sees, leaving a profit of at least £2000 a year to the Exchequer. This was a policy to which Cranmer and Ridley were adamantly opposed, not because they wished to preserve episcopal living standards but because they believed that the church needed these resources to carry out its duties. Zealous as he was for the royal supremacy, by 1552 the archbishop had come to believe that the church needed to retain a degree of autonomy. If episcopal revenues were to be reduced. it should be for the benefit of education, or the enhancement of poor livings, not for the treasury, or to reward the secular aristocracy. Knox and Hooper became disillusioned with their erstwhile patron when they began to appreciate the true motivation behind the campaign of disendowment, and they reacted with the anger of men who feel they have been duped.

The second good reason for Warwick's apparent radical proclivities was his need to retain the king's confidence. Edward's protestantism presumably originated with his tutors, and must have gone back before his father's death, although there is no explicit proof of that. He was making jokes about his sister Mary's conservatism before he had reached his tenth birthday, **27** and there is abundant evidence for the strength of his convictions well before the onset of his final illness. Mary pretended as late as 1552 that her brother was a child who could not yet know his own mind in such matters. In defying the council's religious policy, she repeatedly asserted her willingness to obey the king 'in all things', but only after he had achieved his majority. She may have been deceiving herself, but in all probability she was playing somewhat desperately for time, knowing her position to be untenable. Edward was fond of his sister, but deeply offended by her obstinacy, and the tough stand which Warwick adopted against her non-conformity had his full support, a fact which Mary could not afford to admit. The king was earnest in his devotions, particularly in his attendance at sermons, and took his charitable duties with great seriousness. Specific intervention, apart from his later dealings with his sister, are hard to identify, but it seems that he was personally responsible for the appointment of John Bale to the Irish see of Ossory, and for the council's arbitrary insertion of the Black Rubric into the prayer book. It may well be that Warwick eventually encouraged these radical tendencies in order to wean Edward away from the influence of Cranmer, who was the only man able to challenge him in the king's affections. The Earl's aim was not to dominate, which might have ended in revulsion, but to establish a bond of affection and shared ideals which would endure for the forseeable future. His promotion of the second Prayer Book, the Forty Two Articles, and the campaign against altars can all be seen in this context. The confiscation of 'superfluous' church goods, on the other hand, was not his work, and we have no idea how Edward himself regarded it. Warwick's relations with Cranmer finally broke down over the reformed code of canon law which the archbishop had prepared under the terms of a royal commission. When it was submitted for parliamentary approval in March 1553 Warwick, by that time Duke of Northumberland refused to allow it to be considered on the grounds that it was an infringement of the king's prerogative. By that time the king was ill; but not so ill that his reaction to such an important development could be ignored. Like his father, he had become acutely sensitive to anything which might diminish his authority, or take any aspect of ecclesiastical jurisdiction out of his annointed hands.

Although the affairs of the church touched him most nearly Edward took a keen interest in many other aspects of public affairs. His *Journal* reveals a boyish enthusiasm for jousts and other forms of robust entertainment. He was passionately interested in guns and battles, and enjoyed making lists of information. Technical debates on the reform of the coinage and the collection of revenue were reflected in some of his exercises, and he loved rehersing his entry upon the greater stage of European statesmanship. The first step in Warwick's foreign policy as the head of council was to end the war with France. He was unsentimental about Boulogne, in spite of his role in its capture. It was an expensive white elephant, not worth the cost of maintaining, let alone the crippling expense of a war to defend it. Once he had strengthened his bargaining hand during the winter of 1549/50 by making it clear to Henry II that the town would not be easy to capture, he was prepared to negotiate. Using a Florentine resident in London, Antonio Guidotti, as an intermediary, he began to make delicate soundings before Christmas. Henry responded almost at once. Apart from Boulogne, England was a sideshow and he was anxious to clear the decks for his next round with the Habsburgs. Hints began to be dropped about a more positive improvement in relations, and the possibility of a marriage between Edward and one of the young Valois princesses.

Warwick was cautious. Such a commitment would have meant finally abandoning the treaty of Greenwich; realistic, perhaps, but unpalatable if Boulogne was also to be surrendered. The English commissioners were led by Lord Paget, who had the double advantage of being desperately anxious to please after his brush with conspiracy in December, and expendable if things should go wrong. He was also a very skilful negotiator, and the treaty was secured by the end of March. Boulogne was to be returned to France for 200,000 crowns down, and another 200,000 in August. This was far more than Henry had been willing to pay, and represented about £180, 000 - more than a years ordinary revenue. The Scottish issue was by passed and there was no mention of a marriage, nor of any positive alliance. Instead both kings spoke generally about their 'amity' and mutual goodwill. Neither Warwick nor Paget ever received much credit for this treaty, but it was warmly welcomed at the time and enabled the English council to keep its options open in foreign policy. Once the war with France was ended, Warwick could safely cut his losses in Scotland, and did so later in 1550. It was an inglorious but sensible retreat, which enabled the Scottish protestants to grow into a formidable anti-French force without the contamination of English associations.

Van der Delft worried about the Treaty of Boulogne, and indeed Anglo-Imperial relations continued to be difficult, partly because of the vexed question of the Princess Mary's mass, and partly because of the tactlessness of the English ambassador to Charles's court, Sir Richard Morison, who preached at the Emperor, and tried to demand the right to have protestant services celebrated in his residence.**28** Nevertheless it would be a mistake to see Warwick's policy as simply one of friendship with France and a chilly hostility to the Habsburgs.

The English and French did not trust each other. The French suspected, with some justification, that English dependence upon the great market and bourse at Antwerp would sooner or later drag them back to a Habsburg alliance, and the English feared that Henry II was only dissembling until he could lay his hands on Calais. In a sense both were right, but Warwick also knew that one of the best ways to get a better response from Charles was to make a show of friendship with his great rival, so there was also an element of play acting about Anglo-French relations. This can be seen in the summer of 1551, when the two kings exchanged orders of chivalry. Edward was enchanted with the Marshal St.Andre who came to bestow the order of St.Michael upon him, and whose charm offensive caused sleepless nights in Brussels. At the same time the previously canvassed marriage treaty was also signed, betrothing Edward to the young princess Elizabeth, Henry's daughter. However, such ceremonious gestures of frienship were not very substantial. Edward was approaching his fourteenth birthday, but Elizabeth was far too young for marriage, and there was no question of her being sent to England. Nor was there any mention of a military alliance, or a pledge to defend each others territories. The king enjoyed his introduction to international 'courtesy', and improved his somewhat tongue tied French in the process, but he did not end up committed to anything which could not be conveniently shed, and his council continued to keep both parties at an arms length. Warwick was above all concerned to avoid any further war, and in that he was completely successful.

This was not pusillanimity but common sense. Both Henry VIII and the Protector had spent extravagantly. Henry had taxed extremely hard, and both had debased the coinage, with disastrous consequences for the economy and the exchange rate. By 1551 the debt stood at over £250,000 and the pound sterling stood at 50% of its 1545 rate against the pound flemish. Warwick realised from the start that his first priority, once peace had been acheived, was to ensure that ordinary income covered ordinary expenditure, and he articulated that as a policy in the summer of 1550. It was, however, easier said than done, and at the same time there was over £100,000 owing to the Antwerp bankers. Warwick used some of the first instalment of the French redemption money for Boulogne to ease that burden, but there were many other urgent calls on the money. The City of London was supportive, and indeed without the assistance of the Staplers and the Merchant Adventurers, particularly the latter, the debt problem might well have been insoluble. The first scheme, devised by his friend Sir John Yorke in October 1550 was not only a failure, but led to an acrimonious dispute with the Regent of the Low Countries, Mary of Hungary, over illicit bullion exports. However, after that the situation improved. By 1552 the Merchant Adventurers were regularly using their trading credits to cover government repayments; and Thomas Gresham, one of the acutest financial minds of his generation, became first an unofficial adviser and then the king's agent in Antwerp. By the end of the reign he had restored the pound sterling to its pre-1545 level. There was a price to be paid for this support, and in February 1552 the council was forced to abrogate the long standing privileges of the Hanseatic League, against whom the Adventurers had been pursuing a long feud.(29) This upset the Emperor, whose subjects most of them were, but not badly enough to disrupt the Antwerp trade. Warwick's grasp of financial matters was a little like his grasp of theology - very slender. However he had the sense to leave such matters largely in the hands of those who understood them better, particularly the Earl of Wiltshire and Thomas Gresham. Wiltshire was no financial genius. but he did have a sound strategy of retrenchment, and he understood the importance of getting inflation under control. Prices had risen over 100% between 1545 and 1551, an unprecedented and totally misunderstood process which added greatly to popular anger and confusion. By the autumn of 1551 the disastrous process of debasement had been brought to an end, the base coin had been 'cried down' in value by 25%, and good coin was being minted. Unfortunately the 'crying down' was mishandled, and the council concluded that it could not afford to redeem the base coin before issuing the good. This meant that most of the good coin immediately disappeared, but the inflationary process was checked, and that helped a measure of stability to return to the market. Bad debt and inefficient revenue collection was a constant problem for Tudor governments, and in 1552 the council set up a commission with sweeping powers to investigate the revenue system and to make recommendation, for improvement. The result was an impressive and comprehensive report, but very little immediate action.[30] Military expenditure, one of the commissions main targets, was largely confined to the navy and the garrisons of Berwick and Calais, but the sweeping reductions suggested could not be implemented in the uncertain international situation then prevailing. The main achievements of John Dudley's years in power were the reduction of the overall Crown debt from about £260,000 to about £180,000 and the ingenious manipulations of Thomas Gresham in Antwerp which restored confidence there and enabled Edward to borrow money at 12-14% when both Henry II and the Emperor were paying far more. It was by sixteenth century standards a successful period of financial management.

Peace abroad made a measure of financial recovery possible, and that in turn improved the prospects for domestic stability after the alarming upheavals of 1548/9. The atmosphere remained tense throughout 1550 and 1551. There was much talk of another' camping summer', and bitter complaints against the tyranny and ambition of the Earl of Warwick. Men professed to see his badge of the bear and ragged staff all over the place, from the gates of Norwich to the latest issue of testons, and the council was constantly busied with police work. However, in spite of the alarms the situation was successfully contained. Warwick carefully refrained from giving any further encouragement to the 'commonwealth' lobby, and the reformers themselves fell quiet, alarmed by the storms which they had inadvertently helped to stir up. There was no explicit rejection of their platform, partly because it was shared by a number of prominent protestant preachers, such as Hugh Latimer, and partly because the king accepted it as being, to some extent, an expression of his royal duty. Warwick met parliament reluctantly. He may have feared a revival of 'commonwealth' pressure, or he may have been more generally doubtful of his ability to control it. There were two sessions of the first parliament; from 4th November 1549 to 1st February 1550, and from 23 January to 15th April 1552; and a second, very brief, parliament from 1st to 31st March 1553. In the event the council seems to have managed its legislative programme successfully. It was not excessively reactionary, and in some respects was more enlightened than that of Somerset, but it did include the imposition of the second Prayer Book without reference to Convocation, and the dissolution of the see of Durham. Warwick's management tactics were modelled on those of Cromwell. In the last session of the first parliament about 14 members of the House of Commons could be described in some sense as his men and that figure rose to 17 in March 1553. At the same time other councillors and nobles were mobilised to use their patronage on the governments behalf, and a small number of explicitly directive letters were sent out to selected boroughs.

The secret of the council's success in its domestic policies was unity and it may have been because he saw parliaments as potentially divisive that Warwick tried to avoid them. Somerset had fallen partly at least because he had divided the ruling class against itself. The events of 1549 made that easier to avoid in future. Warwick's social policy roughly followed the aristocratic consensus and the council's radical religious policy was swallowed by a largely conservative nobility and gentry as being preferable to giving the commons another excuse to rise up against lawful authority. This deep, and justified, fear of division also explain Warwick's much criticised dealings with the fallen Protector. Somerset had been formally deprived of his office on the 14th January 1550. The details of his submission were completed on the 27th and he was released under a bond of £10,000 to stay within four miles of his residence at Syon. 31 This rustication lasted only about five weeks, because on the 31st March he was again received at court and was re-admitted to the council on the 10th April. Given the catalogue of charges which had seemed to threaten his very life as recently as the middle of December this rehabilitation was truly remarkable. He had lost both his offices and his annuity of 8000 marks but he had suffered no fine or forfeiture and was apparently in a position to resume the threads of his public life. The explanation for this lies in a calculation by the Earl of Warwick. Somerset may have blamed his former friend for his downfall, but he must also have realised that Warwick had rescued him from the revenge of

Wriothesley and Arundel. The hope was that they would now be able to work together, and that Somerset's considerable popular following, and his high standing with the reformers, would support Warwick in those areas where he was most deficient. Similarly, by including Somerset in the council, it was hoped that he would avoid the temptation to become the leader of a 'country' opposition. It was essential that no such opposition leader should emerge. Princess Mary had no appetite for politics, and the remaining conservative magnates were too concerned to keep the lid on popular discontent; but the former Protector could have been a threat. Unfortunately, this eminently sensible programme did not work. The Duke could not reconcile himself to a supporting role; nor could he pretend to be happy with several aspects of the council's policy. The abandonment of Scotland and the rapprochement with France particularly upset him. Within a few months there were rumours that he was intriguing to recover his former powers. In June 1550 Warwick's eldest surviving son. John. Viscount Lisle married Somerset's daughter Anne, and for a few weeks there was a brave show of amity, but it did not last. Part of the problem lay in the fact that some of the Protector's former followers believed that it was in their interest to stir up strife. Sir Ralph Vane and Richard Whalley were two such men who were apprehended and questioned for their attempts to create a following for Somerset against the Earl. How far the Duke encouraged such activities, or was even aware of them, we do not know, but they brought him into serious danger. By February 1551 the Earl of Shrewsbury could report that he had been canvassed as to his views on Warwick and Somerset as rivals for power, and had responded very sensibly that in his view neither could afford to act in such a devisive manner. However, in April it was being rumoured that the Duke would ally with the disgruntled conservatives, and would withdraw to the north to raise forces against the council. It is reasonably certain that Somerset never had any such intention, and that by the summer of 1551 he had given up whatever ambitions he may have had. Nevertheless the rumours acquired a life of their own, and were nourished by the fact that Somerset refused to lie down, or to acquiesce in policies of which he disapproved. He was being obstructive, and was encouraging others to be obstructive. In other circumstances this might have been merely a nuisance, but the stability of the minority government was not strong enough to tolerate it. As John Hayward later wrote

> '...the Duke of Somerset was thought fit to be taken away, whose credit was so great with the common people, that although it sufficed not to beare out any bad attempt of his owne, yet it was of force to cross the evil purposes of others...'[32]

On the 7th October 1551 Sir Thomas Palmer sought out the Earl of Warwick and 'disclosed a conspiracy' to him. The Duke of Somerset was conspiring to murder him, and the Marquis of Northampton, and to raise the City of London against the council. The charge seems to have been entirely fabricated, although whether by Palmer or by Warwick himself is not entirely clear. Warwick, professing horror and astonishment, swiftly convinced the king of his uncle's guilt, and he was arrested on the 16th October at the council board. There then followed a round up of his alleged accomplices, and a discreet propaganda campaign intended to confuse Somerset's many sympathisers. From the evidence which was then collected it is clear that the Duke had at some point conspired Warwick's overthrow. So much was disclosed by the Earl of Arundel in a testament which bears all the marks of truth. This he may have intended to do using parliament rather than an insurrection, but the consequences would have been the same. In a sense he was guilty, but not as charged. He was brought to trial at Westminster Hall on the 1st December, acquitted of High Treason and found guilty of felony.

Although the charges against him were fabricated, Somerset was not as innocent as his sympathisers later tried to claim. He had criticised Warwick almost as irresponsibly as Lord Seymour had criticised him, and the fact that he had failed to raise a party among the lords does not acquit him of the intention to stir up factional strife. Moreover he admitted at his trial that he had assembled armed men. He claimed that they were a small number for his own protection, and not nearly enough to be construed as a threat. That may have been true, but he had still acted in contravention of the Act against unlawful assemblies. Because he had received no order to disband, he was rightly acquitted of treason; but the assembly itself was a felony, and of that he was guilty by his own confession. Moreover the scale and intensity of the demonstrations in London when it was believed that he would be released shook the council severely, and demonstrated beyond any doubt what a disruptive factor he could have become. He had not plotted to murder the Earl of Warwick, nor to raise a rebellion in London, but the verdict against him was technically correct. Nor was it simply the ambition of the Earl of Warwick which destroyed him; it was also Warwick's fully justified determination not to allow the fragile domestic peace of England to be destroyed.

Tudor England had no standing army, and no police force in the modern sense. In normal circumstances order was maintained and the laws enforced by noblemen and gentlemen holding the king's authority by commission, and utilising their own servants and retainers. So nearly had this system broken down, however, that it was considered necessary after 1550 to reinforce it. Licences for reliable supporters of the council to retain extra men were issued in batches from the spring of 1550 onwards. In April 1550 the king noted in his journal that 2300 such retainers had already been licensed, and in the autumn of 1551, when Somerset was in prison and awaiting trial the household guard was substantially augmented with selected retinues, this time at the king's expense. **33** After the surrender of Boulogne the garrison was redeployed, partly to the Scottish border and partly to likely trouble spots within England. The mercenaries who had played such a large part in the victories of Russell and Warwick in 1549 were likewise retained in pay until 1552. After the execution of Somerset the council seems to have felt able to scale down its precautions somewhat. No doubt the desire to save money was also considered, but money had been even shorter in 1551, when no such relaxation was thought to be possible. W.K. Jordan called the whole of this period 'government by fearful men', but their actions were justified by the result. Unlike his namesake and predecessor Edward VI survived, and in spite of the battering which it received, his government remained surprisingly effective. Coercion, or the threat of coercion, cannot alone explain this. Obedience to the king as a religious duty was deeply engrained, and one of the main reasons for the upheavals of the 'camping years' was that many people believed that the king sympathised with their demands for social justice. When they realised that they were regarded as rebels, many of then went home, and the hard core of militants who sustained the two main campaigns numbered only a few thousand. Moreover the stick was accompanied by the carrot.

Both Seymour and Dudley had learned in the days of Thomas Cromwell the power of a well organised patronage system, but as Protector Somerset had made little constructive use of his knowledge. After December 1547 he had neglected the council, and he had made no more peers after the 'accession list'. His failure to retain even Paget as a loyal supporter was at least as much a failure to reward as a failure to consult. It was not so much that Somerset was mean as that he had no particular policy of grants and rewards, and the people who felt beholden to him were least able to make their gratitude tell.

By contrast the Earl of Warwick earned the reputation of one who plundered the king's revenues to enrich himself, his family and his creatures. The charge was only partly justified. Friends such as Lord Clinton and the Marquis of Dorset, or supporters such as Sir John Gates and Sir Thomas Darcy certainly received numerous grants and favours, but many of the grants were in fact preferential purchases rather than gifts, just as many of the favours were opportunities for profit rather than cash or annuities. The king's coffers were not noticeably drained, and when the profits from fines and attainders is taken into account, the balance was fairly even. The fall of Somerset and his immediate associates, such as Sir Michael Stanhope, brought in almost as much as had been granted away over the previous two years. Warwick's own profits were large, but not out of proportion with his status and responsibilities. In May 1550 he received lands in Northumberland and Yorkshire to the value of £660 per annum. This was a gift in fee simple, and probably linked to plan for him to be Warden General of the Marches, which was not pursued at that time. At the very end of the reign. In June 1553 he received a further gift of an estate worth £400 a year, but all the rest of his innumerable transactions were either purchases or exchanges. No doubt the latter were beneficial, but it is often hard to tell whether the margin of gain was significant. After his fall his lands were valued at £4300 per annum, a notable advance on the £1400 which he had been worth in 1546 as Lord Lisle, but less than Somerset, and very much in line with the wealth of other major peers.

Of course not all his wealth was in land. He had probably coveted the Lord Great Mastership of the Household since the death of the Duke of Suffolk in 1545, and in moving the Earl of Wiltshire to the Lord Treasurership in February 1550, he created the vacancy which he was then able to occupy. The fee was only £200 a year, but the opportunities for patronage were immense. The Wardenship of the Marches to which he was appointed in May 1550 would have carried a fee of £1000 per annum, but that was intended to cover the military expenses of the office, and in any case the plan was abandoned two months later. **34** When he did decide to take a grip on the north in October 1551 he was appointed to the Wardenship General at a fee of 2000 marks. That position he occupied for the remainder of the reign, but again the fee was not all profit and his personal finances probably benefited more from the patronage opportunities than from the income itself. What he did do was acquire a number of stewardship in the last year of the reign. These were worth less than £100 a year, but they were virtual sinecures and also carried useful patronage. He also obtained in June 1552 a release of debts owed to the crown. These went back to 1541 and the sum involved was over £2000.**35** His disposable income from fees, annuities, offices and other benefits was probably well in excess of £1000 a year at the time of his fall, and it is not surprising that when his plate and other assets were valued in August 1553 they amounted to over £10,000. Warwick also rewarded himself and others with titles and promotions. As we have seen, several followed his victory over Arundel and Southampton in January 1550; another batch immediately preceded his final strike against the Duke of Somerset in October 1551. William Herbert became Earl of Pembroke William Paulet, Earl of Wiltshire became Marquis of Winchester, Henry Grey; Marquis of Dorset became Duke of Suffolk, and John Dudley himself became Duke of Northumberland, the title by which he is best known to posterity. Far more peers were created during this period than were destroyed. Apart from the Seymour brothers no peer was executed during the whole reign. The former Duke of Norfolk and the heir to the Earldom of Devon remained in the Tower, whence they were to be released by Mary. The Earl of Southampton died, of chagrin it was said, in the summer of 1550, and the Earl of Arundel and Lord Paget were imprisoned and heavily fined for their supposed involvement in Somerset's conspiracy. Paget discharged his debt and was pardoned during 1552, and Arundel had most of his fine remitted. Neither had any affection for the Duke of Northumberland, but they made no disruptive moves as long as Edward lived.

Northumberland's management of the council and the peerage down to July 1553 was remarkably successful. As Dale Hoak demonstrated nearly twenty years ago, he used the council much more positively than the Protector had done. He recruited his friends to it, and excluded potential enemies, but avoided creating a dangerously disaffected 'country' party. Paradoxically his unpopularity with the commons was an advantage in this respect, and it was generally accepted by the aristocracy that his leadership, little as they might like him, was necessary for their own security and the stability of the kingdom.

IX The Fall of the Duke of Northumberland, 1552-1553

Northumberland was defeated eventually by a cruel twist of fate. Having done everything in his power to make sure that he would retain Edward's confidence after 1555, and made a number of enemies in the process, he then found in the early summer of 1553 that the king was dying. Mortality was always uncertain in the sixteenth century, but there had been no warning of the onset of this fatal illness. Edward had not been the sickly child of legend, but remarkably robust - far more so than Northumberland himself. He had escaped the sweating sickness, that lethal and mysterious ailment which had claimed the lives of so many of his subjects duing 1551 and 1552, and had probably contributed to the relative peacefulness of those years in the process. Previous colds and chills he had thrown of with encouraging resilience; but at Christmas 1552 he developed an infection which refused to go away, and which modern medical historians suspect was pulmonary tuberculosis. During January and February the symptoms seemed no more than a temporary nuisance, but on the 1st March he was too ill to open parliament in the nornal way, and his physicians began to be anxious. By the close of the parliament he seemed to be better, and through most of April a normal recovery was expected. It was not until early June that his condition began to deteriorate so rapidly that his life appeared to be seriously threatened. Within a fortnight or so the succession went from being an almost academic matter to being a question of the highest urgency. There need not have been a problem, because the succession act of 1543, confirmed by Henry VIII's will had laid down an order which provided for Edward's death without heirs. In such an event Mary was to succeed, unless she had married without the council's consent, in which case the crown was to pass to her half sister Elizabeth. Unfortunately Edward himself had already rejected such a solution. At some point before he became seriously ill, and long before it became a matter of urgency, probably in January 1553, the king had jotted down some thoughts on the subject.

His so-called 'device' for the succession is a strange document. The order laid down by statute is totally ignored. Neither Mary nor Elizabeth is mentioned, and the proposals begin with the Lady Frances, that is Frances Grey, duchess of Suffolk. She had been born Frances Brandon, and was the daughter of Henry VIII's sister Mary by her second marriage to Charles Brandon. 36 Edward was clearly obsessed with two factors, legitimacy and male succession. He was also desperately anxious to protect the protestant reformation over which he had presided, and which had come to mean so much to him. His rejection of Mary can be explained on grounds of both religion and legitimacy. He knew only too well how strongly she adhered to the old faith, and he also knew how his father had struggled to free himself from her mother. The rejection of Elizabeth is harder to explain, because she shared his faith, and had always appeared to be *persona grata* at court. However, it would appear that he took his father's revulsion against Anne Boleyn just as seriously as that against Catherine. If Elizabeth was the daughter of an incestuous adultress, then she was unworthy of the throne, no matter what statute might say. Moreover both were women and unmarried, presenting just that hazard to the realm which his father had fought so hard to avoid. Consequently Edward's order started, not with Frances herself, but with any male heir which she might subsequently bear. It then proceeded via the male heirs of her three daughters none of whom were yet married, to the male heir of the Lady Margaret Clifford, the daughter of Frances's younger sister Eleanor, who was already dead. None of these boys yet existed, and Frances was probably past the child bearing age, so the time span envisaged was a long one. Having explored all these various avenues briefly, the king's jottings then returned to the possibility that he might die before any of these hypothetical sons appeared. In that event, he suggested, the Lady Frances should act as Guardian of the Realm until such time as one of her daughters bore a son. In other words the monarchy would be put in abeyance for an indefinite period of time. Such a bizarre idea bore no relation to the possibilities of real politics, and indicates that Edward was playing with ideas rather than making serious proposals. It is not clear that anyone else knew about this document at the time. There is no record of it having been discussed, or even alluded to, and no proposal was brought to the parliament in March.

The original document is written in the king's own hand, but because of the use to which it was subsequently put, it has often been suggested that the true author was the Duke of Northumberland. Northumberland, however, was a realist. There was no Salic Law in England, and even Henry VIII had not ventured to act as though there was. Neither he, nor any other responsible councillor would have suggested suspending the monarchy, nor believed that it was possible to do so. When the crisis came at the beginning of June, Edward had to be persuaded to make some other arrangement, and it was at that point that Northumberland's powerful influence was brought to bear. Because of the skill with which he had played his educational cards, the king would listen to him in preference to anyone else, even Cranmer. Whether he tried to persuade Edward to adhere to the statutory order and failed, or whether he saw advantages to himself in the 'device' and did not even try, we do not know. What is clear is that Edward agreed to make the smallest possible alteration to his original instrument in order to bring it into the realms of practical possibility. Bypassing Frances, he bequeathed his throne to 'the Lady Jane and her heirs male'. Jane was Frances's eldest daughter, a girl of sixteen. She was an almost exact contemporary of the king's, had shared some of his schooling, and was as zealous a protestant as himself. If there had to be a female on the throne, then it is not difficult to see why Edward should have favoured her. She was also safely married to an English nobleman, and therefore presented no risk of foreign domination. The fact that her husband was Lord Guildford Dudley, the fourth son of his trusted councillor the Duke of Northumberland, would have been an additional commendation. She also represented the quickest route to a male heir, given that her mother was too old, and her sisters too young.

Jane and Guildford had been married with the king's blessing, on the 21st May 1553, and it has frequently been argued that this was a calculated move on Northumberland's part to bring the crown into his own fanily. However Edward was enjoying his last major remission in late May. His recovery was generally expected. and at no point in his fluctuating illness before that date had his life been despaired of. Jane was the eldest daughter of his ally and friend the Duke of Suffolk, and a natural match for his only unmarried son. At the same time his daughter Catherine married Lord Hastings, the heir to the Earldom of Huntingdon, and Jane's younger sister, also Catherine, married Lord Herbert the son of the Earl of Pembroke. Northumberland obviously knew of Jane's proximity to the succession, but there is no reason to suppose that he believed it to be a matter of great or urgent significance. He was indulging in cementing a series of dynastic alliances, and he may not even have been aware of the 'device' at that stage. As we have seen, Northumberland's eldest son, John, had married Anne Seymour in 1550. Ambrose had already lost his first wife, Anne Whorwood and was currently married to Elizabeth Talbot. Henry's wife was Margaret the daughter of Thomas, Lord Audley; Robert was married to Amy Robsart, the daughter of a substantial Norfolk squire, and Mary was the wife of Henry Sidney. Guildford and Catherine were therefore the last to be bestowed, and their nuptials saw the last stage of a routine paternal duty rather than the first stage of a major political gamble. However, ten days later the king collapsed, and all the plans which the Dudleys had been framing towards the year 1555 were threatened with total ruin.

In the spring of 1553 Northumberland had gone out of his way to be civil to Mary; not, it would seem, because he expected the king's death, but because it was always a good idea to keep on the right side of the heir to the throne, and he knew perfectly well that the princess blamed him, above all, for the religious harassment which she had endured. At that stage, he seems to have had no idea that the king intended to bar his sister and traverse his father's will. However, by the 12th June when Edward sent for his law officers and ordered them to draw up his will on the basis of the revised 'device', he was fully committed. It was a very delicate situation. The king could not simply override a statute *mere moto suo*, nor could Edward, as a minor, make a legally binding will. The law officers wriggled and protested until Northumberland preremptorily ordered them to do the king's bidding, threatening them with physical violence if they refused. It was not a dignified performance, but he could not afford to hedge.

As long as the king was alive, he was owed full obedience, and in the unlikely event of Edward recovering, he would not readily forgive those who had sought to frustrate his will. On the 15th June the king again assembled the officers and his council, and ordered them to set their hands to the 'device'. They oheyed, being advised by Sir Edward Montague that it was manifest treason to refuse the king's explicit command, and comforting themselves with the thought that it was what happened after Edward's death which mattered not what happened before. Nevertheless, when the king's sufferings finally came to an end of the evening of the 6th July, Jane was proclaimed queen and there was at first no dissenting voice, except among the citizens of London.

Northumberland's motivation at this point requires examination, because it was his leadership and commitment which at first held the council together. Had he simply ignored the 'device', which had never been turned into a legally binding instrument in spite of Edward's instructions, and proclaimed Mary queen, there could have been no case against him. On the other hand, he would have been unlikely to enjoy the favour or confidence of the new ruler. Cranmer later testified that he had disapproved of the proclamation of Jane, but adhered to it beccause he had sworn an oath to do so.[37] It would be cynical to suppose that Dudley, and indeed others, would not have taken their oaths with equal seriousness. At the same time he knew the strength of feeling with which Edward had regarded the issue, and may well have felt bound by his word to the dying boy. In the circumstances such a reaction would not have been discreditable. Not being a lawyer, it is probable that Northumberland did not take the constitutional point about the authority of statute very seriously. Other things being equal he would have obeyed the provisions of Henry VIII's will, but other things were not equal. We do not really know whether he shared any of the convictions which had caused Edward to act as he did; whether he was obeying the king, or simply humouring him. Once Edward was dead both conscience and ambition could have prompted him to act as he did. It is also relevant to notice that just about every observer of the events of July 1553 thought at first that he would succeed. Even the Emperor's special ambassadors, sent across to monitor the situation, reported in the second week of July that the Duke had all the resources of the kingdom at his command. 38 Mary had proclaimed herself queen in Norfolk, but deeply as they regretted it, they considered that she had no chance, and their own instructions were not to interfere. The French ambassador, Antoine de Noailles, fearing that Mary would be simply an Imperial puppet, had already offered his master's assistance to Northumberland, but the latter had assured him that he had already taken sufficient precautions against the princess's challenge.

Two factors frustrated this self assurance, and led to his ruin. The first was the speed and efficiency with which Mary moved, and the second was his own lack of old fashioned 'manred'. Surprising as it might seem to anyone who knew Mary's history, with its long catalogue of dithering and hysterics, she was ready for the crisis provoked by her brother's death. It was her clear duty to claim her royal inheitance, and when Mary's conscience spoke clearly, she obeyed it, no matter what the cost. Moreover she had an undistinguished but loyal affinity of East Anglian gentry who were prepared to fight for her cause, should that be necessary. During the last few weeks of Edward's life that affinity was mobilised, although whether by Mary herself or by someone on her behalf, we do not know. Proclamations and letters of summons were drawn up in anticipation of the event and dozens of gentlemen stood by, with men, money and supplies, ready to move at a few hours notice. Northumberland, by contrast had few men of his own. In theory he commanded the household troops, the garrison of the Tower, the fleet, and the retinues of his allies and fellow councillors. But none of these owed their first loyalty to him, and the mercenaries who had once served him had been disbanded. Confidence was as critical to the confrontation which followed as it is to the modern stock market. Had Mary hesitated, or not provided firm leadership, her chance would have slipped away, because the vast majority of the aristocracy and many towns, sat gingerly on the fence waiting to see which way the wind would blow. The princess proclaimed herself queen as soon as the news of Edward's death was confirmed on the 6th July, and wrote at once to the council, claiming their allegiance. Within 24 hours armed men were gathering at Kenninghall, and her proclamations were being read in the neighbouring counties.

The council promptly rejected her claim, but in other respects reacted with a notable lack of urgency, merely writing the customary circular letter to sheriffs and JPs, informing them of Jane's accession, and instructing them to suppress any 'stirs'. Several East Anglian towns originally declared for Jane, but the efforts of Lord Robert Dudley in the countryside were largely unsupported. By the 12th July Mary had several thousand men under arms, and no move had been made against her. At the same time she had no captain of skill or experience, certainly no one capable of matching the Duke of Northumberland. The Duke was then faced with a choice. Either he could go against Mary with whatever men he had available, and trust to his reputation to outface her superior numbers, or he could stay in London, gathering his strength, and making sure that his colleagues stayed in line. He chose the former, deeming that the rapid expansion of Mary's force, and the fact that substantial gentlemen and nobles were now joining her represented the chief danger. In the event he was probably wrong. Advancing too boldly into a hostile country, and bombarded with rumours of the vast size of Mary's host, by the time he got to Cambridge his men were beginning to desert. That setback alone he might have survived, falling back on London and adopting an alternative strategy. However as soon as his back was turned the council began to divide, and it was swiftly revealed that Jane's claim had no committed backing in any sector of the community. Simon Renard, the leader of the Imperial mission claimed the credit for bringing this about by pretending to have secured evidence proving that Jane Grey was merely a front for the French backed claim of Mary Queen of Scots. However the truth seems to have been that several councillors had accepted Jane only with reluctance, believing Mary to be incapable of making good her claim. Her resolute stand, combined with the fact that Northumberland's campaign had ground to a halt, gave them the confidence to display their hand. On the 19th July the defectors proclaimed Mary in London amid overwhelming rejoicing. All those who were not hopelessly compromised hastened to Framlingham to submit to the new queen, and Northumberland with a handful of followers, was left stranded.

From a historical distance it looks as though Mary had an easy victory, but contemporary outsiders were flabbergasted, and in fact it had been a close call. If the radical protestants had not been alienated by his 'worldliness' if he had stayed in London after 13th July, or if he had had a couple of thousand reliable men, the outcome might have been different. It is misleading to speak simply of the 'legitimism' of the English, or their religious conservatism, or even of Northumberland's unpopularity as being the main causes of Mary's success. The actual outcome was determined by human courage and human error. Northumberland's most serious error had been to rely on offices and money rather than men. Apart from his own family, there was hardly anyone who was prepared to stand with him in adversity and no 'country' for him to retreat into or appeal to. Once he had lost his grip over the crown and the machinery of central government, he was as powerless as a modern prime minister who has lost a vote of confidence. To that extent the feudal trappings of nobility, great estates and a huge household are misleading. Northumberland was not a tribal chieftain, even to the same extent as the Earl of Derby or the Earl of Pembroke. He was a politician, and there is no doubt that, if he had been given the chance, he would have served Mary with the same self-seeking diligence that he had deployed in the service of her predecessors. Unfortunately for him, Mary had rather more conventional ideas.

Having made his own gesture of proclaiming Mary at Cambridge Northumberland simply waited with a handful of servants and followers for whatever should transpire. Flight does not seem to have occurred to him. Perhaps he was a fatalist, or perhaps he believed that in some incomprehensible manner he could turn the situation around. He may even have deceived himself into believing that Mary, who had no 'shadow council' would be unable to manage without his experience of affairs. He surrendered to the Earl of Arundel on the 24th July, and was lodged in the Tower the following day. During the week which followed about 30 peers and gentlemen were also arrested for their part in Jane's brief usurpation. Having won a bloodless victory, and in the euphoria of believing that God had worked a miracle on her behalf, Mary was not inclined to be vindictive. Most of those arrested were questioned and released before the middle of August including, very surprisingly, the Duke of Suffolk. But the queen had no intention of forgiving the Dudleys. It was convenient and congenial to blame the Duke, not only for the attempt to crown Jane Grey, but also for the religious policy of the last four years, which she found so deeply abhorent. Her brother, for whom she had a deep personal affection, remained for her a deluded child, manipulated by wicked men, of whom John Dudley was the chief. She had always been inclined to see life in simple terms of black and white, and had no interest in discovering the real nature of Edward's personality. Northumberland, his son the Earl of Warwick and the Marquis of Northampton were tried by the court of the High Steward on the 18th of August. Warwick and Northampton offered no defence, but the Duke argued that he had done nothing but what was approved under the great seal of England, and, with a touch of bitterness, that if he had offended, then most of his judges shared his guilt. Such protests were a waste of breath, because the seal of a usurper had no validity in law and the composition of the court was a political matter. All three were condemned, and were granted a gentleman's death by decapitation. Northumberland also asked to speak with members of the council about matters of state, and to confess to a learned divine.

The Duke's brother, Sir Andrew, his remaining sons, Ambrose, Henry and Robert, and a small group of his followers were tried separately and also condemned. Jane, Guildford and Archbishop Cranmer shared the same fate a few weeks later. Of those convicted only Northumberland himself, Sir John Gates and Sir Thomas Palmer actually suffered at the time, although the sentences on Jane and Guildford were carried out subsequently as a result of the Wyatt rising. Attention, however, remained focussed on Northumberland, whose extraordinary behaviour in the four days between his trial and his execution on the 22nd August attracted fascinated attention, both at the time and since. It seems that his dignified comportment at his trial continued to cover a conviction that he could redeem his situation. He failed to convince the council of his indispensability, but the divine to whom he confessed was Stephen Gardiner, who had suffered deprivation and several years of imprisonment at his hands. Gardiner may have been particularly persuasive, or Northumberland may have believed that the failure of his plans was a message from God about the error of his ways; or (as is usually believed) he decided to make one final bid to save his life and placate the queen. He let it be known that he was prepared to make a public renunciation of protestantism. His execution, originally scheduled for the 21st, was put back and he was paraded in front of a distinguished audience in the chapel of the Tower. There, after hearing mass and receiving the sacrament, he told the assembled congregation:-

> 'Truly I profess here before you all that I have received the sacrament according to the true catholic faith; and the plagues that is upon the realm and upon us now is that we have erred from the faith these sixteen years. And this I profess unto you all from the bottom of my heart...'**39**

His submission, we are told, edified his hearers greatly. However it availed nothing to save his life, and effectually prevented any rehabilitation of his reputation when the protestants recovered the ascendancy under Elizabeth. What he really believed we do not know, and perhaps he did not know himself. Whatever faith he had had no deep intellectual or emotional roots, and in the last crisis of his life he may simply have reverted to the certainties of his childhood.

Later that same day the Lieutenant of the Tower warned him to prepare for death, and he realised that his gamble, if such it was, had failed. In obvious agony of mind he sat down and wrote to his old enemy the Earl of Arundel, begging for his last minute intercession.

> 'Alas my good lord, is my crime so heynous as no redemption but my blood can wash away the spots thereof?.. And if my life be lengthened by your medication and my good Lord Chancellors... I will vow it to be spent at your honourable feet..' **40**

It was an understandable but undignified act of self abasement, and totally useless. Even if Arundel had been prepared to do his best, there was no chance that the queen would have relented. On the morning of the 22nd of August, Northumberland, Gates and Palmer were brought to the scaffold on Tower Green. The latter spoke briefly, acknowledging his faults and admitting that his zeal for the reformed faith had been a sham. The Duke, as befitted the principal actor in the drama, made a longer oration, which was duly taken down and subsequently published in a number of different versions. It was a composed and a very proper performance:

> 'Indeed I confess unto you that I have been an evil liver and have done wickedly all the days of my life...'

This was the sort of thing that condemned men were suppposed to say, admitting the justice of the sentence against them, and urging virtue and obedience upon their hearers. Apart from the fact that he reaffirmed his submission to the catholic church, there was little of interest in his scaffold speech. Having devoted his whole life to making his fortune in the service of the Crown, he died a traitor and few tears were shed for him, either then or since.

The only person who seems to have been genuinely distressed by his death was his widow, Jane, who had been his devoted and almost totally silent shadow for nearly thirty years. She was not charged with any offence, and does not seem to have been imprisoned. She retained control of her jointure lands, and enjoyed the benefit of some enfoeffments to use which the Duke had made on her behalf. She spent the summer of 1554 haunting the court, trying to obtain mercy for her imprisoned sons, and received many kindnesses, both from the queen herself and also from some of Philip's Spanish followers. In early October, the Earl of Warwick was released, but he was already mortally sick and died on the 21st. Robert, Ambrose and Henry were freed in January 1555 and subsequently pardoned, but their mother did not live to see their partial rehabilitation. She died on the 15th of January, at her house in Chelsea, aged forty six. The three surviving Dudleys recieved modest grants from the crown, and served in the French war of 1557-9, but were never in favour. Henry was killed at St.Quentin in 1557, but Ambrose and Robert survived to enjoy distinguished careers in the service of Elizabeth. Neither had any legitimate offspring, and the direct line of the family came to an end in 1590. Northumberland's goods were inventoried by commission in September 1553, and sold off or distributed by the queen's favour. His household of over 200 servants was paid off, and for the time being the Dudleys disappeared below the political horizon. Restoration of the family fortunes after 1558 brought back together some of the Duke's former friends and servants in the affinities of his sons, particularly the Earl of Leicester, but Robert never made any attempt to recreate his father's career. He did not even take any great pains to restore his reputation. In a culture increasingly shaped by John Foxe's *Acts and Monuments*, no apostate could ever be a hero.

Consequently John Dudley's enemies had the field to themselves until about twenty years ago, when the stereotype began to be broken down. We are now in a position to form a much more balanced view about what sort of a man he was, & what inspired his career. He was both more honest and more skilful than he has often been given credit for, and in power he was an effective chief executive. The extent of his achievement, however, beyond the building of his own career, remains problematical. He was probably most successful as Lord Admiral, completing the building of Henry VIII's navy, and giving it both an efficient administrative structure and a modern concept of tactics. Although he was Admiral for only a few months under Edward, the momentum of naval development was sustained. He also encouraged the merchants of London to look beyond their traditional markets, and helped to set up the first voyages of discovery, which set off in 1553 to seek the north east passage. These aspects of his activities probably give him the best claim to be described as a man of vision. However it must also be remembered that he held the minority government of Edward VI together from 1550 to 1553, and enabled it to survive a period of acute financial and social stress which could have inflicted much greater damage than it did. Equally important, although quite inadvertent on his part, was his failure in 1553 to uphold the clearly expressed wishes of the king against the power of statute. The constitutional future of England probably owed at least as much to his failure as to his success.

Notes and References

1. *Acts of the Privy Council*, ed. J R Dasent et al. (London 1890-1907), III, p.347.
2. D M Brodie, 'Edmund Dudley; Minister of Henry VII', *Transactions of the Royal Historical Society*, 1932, pp.133-47. The Anglica Historia of Polydore Vergil, ed. Denys Hay, *Camden Series,* 74, 1950, p.133.
3. Statute 3 Henry VIII, c.19. *Statutes of the Realm*, III,p.
4. Edward Hall, *The Union of the Two Noble and Illustre Houses of York and Lancaster* (Chronicle), ed. 1-1. Ellis (London 1809) p. 671. British Library Add. MS 10110, f.236.
5. According to the Dudley Pedigree their third son, John was born in 1528. The eldest, Henry, died in 1544 and the second, Thomas, probably in infancy. BL. Stowe MS 652.
6. *Letters and Papers...of the Reign of Henry VIII*, ed J Gairdner et al. (London 1862-1932), V. 119 (52)
7. *Letters and Papers*, III, 601.
8. *Letters and Papers*, XV11,163; BL Add. MS 46354, f.2.
9. *Letters and Papers*, XVII, 1048.
10. *Letters and Papers*, XVIII, 450, 451.
11. *Letters and Papers*, XIX, ii, 337.
12. The Sieur d'Ecke, a member of the Emperor's council, 24th August 1545. *Letters and Papers*, XX, ii, 203.
13. *Acts of the Privy Council*, II, pp.4-5.
14. Van der Delft to the Emperor, 8th February 1549; *Calendar of State Papers*, Spanish, ed. R Tyler et al. (London 1862- 1954), IX, p.340.
15. Public Record Office E318/2042.
16. PRO SP10/4, no.26.
17. Deposition of John Fowler. PRO SP10/6, no.10.

18 Historical Manuscripts Commission, *Bath MSS at Longleat.* De Lisle and Dudley Papers, I, f.20.
19 BL Add. MS 48126, ff.6v-16v; partly published by A J A Malkiewicz as 'An eye witness account of the coup d'etat of October 1549', in the *English Historical Review,* 70, 1955.
20 Van der Delft to the Emperor, 15th September 1549; *Cal. Span.*, IX, p.248.
21 Richard Grafton, *Chronicle at Large* (ed. London 1809), II, p.522.
22 John Stow, *The Annales of England* (London 1615), p.598.
23 *The Chronicle and Political Papers of Edward VI,* ed. W K Jordan (London 1970), p.18.
24 'The Letters of Richard Scudamore to Sir Philip Hoby, September 1549 - March 1555', ed. Susan Brigden, *Camden Miscellany,* 30, 1990, pp.95-9.
25 BL Add. MS 48126, ff, 15v-16r. D E Hoak, *The King's Council in the Reign of Edward VI,* (Cambridge 1976), p.255.
26 P L Hughes and J F Larkin, *Tudor Royal Proclamations,* (New Haven, Conn. 1964-69), I, pp.485-6.
27 When Thomas Seymour raised the question of his marriage with the king early in 1547, the boy had advised that he should 'marry my sister Mary, to turn her opinions'. PRO SP10/6. no.10.
28 Emperor to Jehan Scheyfve, 7th March 1551, *Cal Span.*, X, pp.238-41.
29 *Acts of the Privy Council,* III, pp.487-9; 24th February 1552.
30 W C Richardson, *The Report of the Royal Commission of 1552,* (Morganstown, Va. 1974). J D Alsop, The Revenue Commission of 1552, *Historical Journal,* 22, 1979,

pp.511-33.
31 Stow, *Annales*, pp.602-3; *Cal.Span.*, X, p.28.
32 John Hayward, *The Life and Raigne of King Edward the Sixth*, ed. B L Beer, (Kent, Ohio, 1993) p.137.
33 They were mustered on December 7th, just after the trial. Edward VI, *Chronicle*, p.100.
34 *Calendar of the Patent Rolls*, III, p.406. *Acts of the Privy Council,* III, p.88.
35 *Cal Pat.*, IV p.347.
36 Inner Temple, Petyt MS xlviii, f.316, printed and edited in J G Nichols, *Literary Remains of King Edward VI* (London, 1857) II,PP.571-2.
37 Cranmer to the Queen, December 1553; *The Works of Thomas Cranmer*, ed. J E Cox (London 1844-6), II, p.442.
38 Ambassadors to the Emperor, 12th July 1553; *Cal Span.*, XI, p.85.
39 B L Harley MS 284, f128v; *The Greyfriars Chronicle of London,* ed J G Nichols (Camden Society 1852), p.83.
40 B L Harley MS 787, f.61v.

Suggestions for Further Reading

A: BOOKS

B L Beer:*Northumberland; the political career of John Dudley, Earl of Warwick and Duke of Northumberland* (Kent, Ohio, 1973)
M L Bush:*The Government Policy of Protector Somerset* (Manchester, 1975)
S E Brigden:*London and the Reformation* (Oxford, 1989)
C E Challis:*The Tudor Coinage* (Manchester, 1978)
J Cornwall:*The Revolt of the Peasantry, 1549* (London 1977)

S Gammon:*Statesman and Schemer; William, First Lord Paget of Beaudesert* (Newton Abbot, 1973)
S J Gunn:*Charles Brandon, Duke of Suffolk, 1484-1545* (Oxford, 1988)
D E Hoak:*The King's Council in the Reign of Edward VI* (Cambridge, 1976)
W Jordan:*Edward VI: the Young King* (London 1968)
W Jordan:*Edward VI: The Threshold of Power* (London 1970)
S K Land:*Kett's Rebellion* (Ipswich, 1977)
J Loach :*Protector Somerset* (Bangor, 1994)
D Loades:*Mary Tudor: a Life* (Oxford, 1989)
D Loades:*Lectures on the Reign of Edward VI* (Bangor 1994)
D Loades:*John Dudley, Duke of Northumberland 1504-1553*
D MacCulloch:*Thomas Cranmer* (Yale, 1996)
H Miller:*Henry VIII and the English Nobility* (Oxford 1986)
G Redworth:*In Defence of the Church Catholic; the Life of Stephen Gardiner* (Oxford 1990)
W Richardson:*The Report of the Royal Commission of 1552* (Morganstown, Va., 1-974)
L Smith :*Henry VIII: the Mask of Royalty* (London, 1971)
C Sturge:*Cuthbert Tunstall* (London, 1938)
D Wilson:*Sweet Robin: a biography of Robert Dudley, Earl of Leicester* (London, 1981)

B: ARTICLES

S Adams: 'The Dudley Clientele, 1553-1563', in *The Tudor Nobility*, ed. G W Bernard, Manchester, 1992.
J D Alsop:'The Revenue Commission of 1552', *Historical Journal*, 22. 1979. pp. 511-33.
G Bernard:'The Downfall of Sir Thomas Seymour' in *The Tudor Nobility*

B L Beer: 'Northumberland: the myth of the wicked Duke and the historical John Dudley', *Albion*, 8, 1987, pp.1-11

R Braddock:'The character and compostion of the Duke of Northumberland's army', *Albion*, 8 1987, pp.1-11

D Brodie'Edmund Dudley: minister of Henry VII', *Transactions of the Royal Historical Society*, 4th series, 15, 1932, pp.133-47

M L Bush'The problems of the far north, *Northern History*, 6, 1971

J Cornwall &:'Debate: Kett's rebellion in context', *Past and*
D.MacCulloch *Present*, 93, 1981 pp.160-73

C S Davies:'Slavery and Protector Somerset; the Vagrancy Act of 1547', *Economic History Review*, 2nd series 19, 1966

G R Elton: 'Thomas Cromwell's decline and fall', in *Studies in Tudor and Stuart Politics and Government*; I, Cambridge 1974, pp.189-230

F Emmison: 'A plan of Edward VI and Secretary Petre for reorganising the Privy Council's work, 1552-3',*Bulletin of Historical Research* 1, 1958, pp.203-7

S J Gunn 'The Duke of Suffolk's march on Paris in 1523', *English Historical Review*, 101, 1986, pp.596-634

C J Harrison:'The petition of Edmund Dudley', *English Historical Review*, 87, 1971, pp.82-99

D E Hoak 'Rehabilitating the Duke of Northumberland; Politics and Political Control, 1549-1553', in J Loach and R Titler, eds., *The Mid-Tudor Polity, 1540-1560*, London, 1980, pp.29-51

D E Hoak: 'The King's Privy Chamber, 1547-1553', in D J.Guth and J McKenna, eds., *Tudor Rule and Revolution,* Cambridge, 1982. pp. 87-198

D E Hoak: 'The Secret History of the Tudor Court, the King's Coffers and the King's Purse, 1542-1553', in C Coleman and D Starkey, eds., *Revolution Reassessed,* London, 1986, pp.87-115

M Horowitz: 'Richard Empson, minister of Henry VII' *Bulletin of the Institute of Historical Research,* 55, 1982, pp.35-49

E W Ives: 'Henry VIII's Will: a forensic conundrum', *Historical Journal,* 35, 1992

H James: 'The aftermath of the 1549 coup and the Earl of Warwick intentions', *Historical Research,* 62, 1989

D Loades: 'The dissolution of the diocese of Durham, 1553-4', in *Politics, Censorship and the English Reformation,* 1991, pp. 167-79

A Malkiewicz: 'An eyewitness account of the coup d'etat of October 1549', *English Historical Review,* 70, 1955, pp.600-09

J Murphy: 'The illusion of decline; the Privy Chamber, 1547-1558', in *The English Court from the Wars of the Roses to the Civil War,* ed. D Starkey, London, 1987, pp.119-146.

H Miller: 'Henry VIII's unwritten will; grants of land and honours in 1547', in E W Ives, R J Knecht and J J Scarisbrick eds., *Wealth and Power in Tudor England,* London 1978, pp.87-10s

A Slavin: 'The fall of Lord Chancellor Wriothesley: a study in the politics of conspiracy', *Albion,* 7, 1975,pp.265-85

P Slack: 'Social policy and the constraints of government', in *The Mid-Tudor Polity*, pp.94-115

R Somerville: 'Henry VII's council Learned in the Law ', *English Historical Review*, 54, 1939, pp.427-42

W Tighe: 'The gentlemen pensioners, the Duke of Northumberland and the attempted coup of 1553', *Albion*, 19, 1987, pp.1-11.

R Tittler &
D Battley :'The local community and the Crown in 1553;the accession of Mary Tudor revisted', *Bulletin of the Institute of Historical Research*, 136, 1984,pp.131-40

J Youings: 'The South Western Rebellion of 1549', *Southern History*, 1, 1979, pp.x9-122

G J Parry: 'Inventing the Good Duke of Somerset', *Journal of Ecclesiastical History*, 40, 1989